To my dad, Dennis, and Liz's mom, Sherla

100 Recipes That
Redefine Outdoor Cooking

Symon's Dinners
Cooking
Out

Michael Symon
and Douglas Trattner
Photographs by Ed Anderson

Clarkson Potter/Publishers | New York

Contents

Introduction

Every cookbook that I've written has been a labor of love, and this one is no different. Even though the recipes change, as does the theme, what remains consistent from book to book is the approach we have when starting out. From the moment I first start jotting down notes and ideas, the goal of each cookbook is to help people live a more delicious life. Sometimes that's by offering up quick and easy dishes that can be made with five fresh ingredients (*Michael Symon's Five in Five*), other times it's by producing the very best live-fire cookbook on store shelves (IMHO . . . *Playing with Fire*), or maybe it's about sharing recipes and a game plan for cooks dealing with inflammation issues like me who don't want to sacrifice flavor and joy in their meals (*Fix It with Food*).

No matter what the subject, I am proud of every cookbook that I've put out—I'm looking at you, *Simply Symon Suppers*! That said, this one occupies a special place in my heart. Its genesis stretches all the way back to Day 1 of the lockdown in 2020. That's when we had the crazy idea to start filming live cooking shows in my home kitchen. I know it feels like ancient history now, but those were such crazy times, when restaurants were closed or just doing takeout and many ingredients were not available at local grocery stores. So, Liz, Olivia, and I turned to the iPhone camera and began shooting unscripted one-hour cooking shows that relied on a combination of basic ingredients and pantry staples. Because they streamed live, people could type in questions to be answered in real time, with rambunctious little Norman the puppy romping in the background. At a time when the only news around felt like bad news, those shows managed to foster a real sense of community and give people something to look forward to. I know they did for me and my family.

Thanks to the incredible team at Food Network who pushed the content out across all of their social media channels, we quickly developed a massive following for those unconventional cooking shows. Those early #SymonDinners evolved into *Symon's Dinners Cooking Out,* which took the freewheeling party out of the kitchen and into the backyard. What started in the summer of 2020, with me, Liz, and Liv doing our thing, is still a Food Network hit.

When I'm cooking outside—filming or not—the last thing I want to do is split my time between my indoor kitchen and the grill. I truly believe that anything that can be made inside can be made outside on a standard charcoal grill. Yes, I will admit that it might be easier to do some things indoors, like boiling water for pasta or baking a finicky cake, but where is the fun and adventure in that?!

The number one thing that I love about cooking—and why I have devoted my life to it—is that food brings people together. It did with *Simply Symon Suppers* and it does with *Symon's Dinners Cooking Out,* and it will when you gather family and friends in the backyard and prepare the recipes in this book, from easy starters to pasta, steak, and cake, all made on the grill.

Hey, I'm not crying, you're crying!

Much love to all!
MS

Get Grilling

Basic Grill Setups

Most of the recipes in this book call for a direct-heat setup or an indirect-heat setup. There are a few exceptions, like when a recipe calls for unusually long and low-heat cooks. In those instances, the snake or minion methods are ideal because they eliminate the need to replenish briquettes. Let's break them down, shall we?

Direct-Heat Setup

With the **direct-heat setup**, all of the coals are spread out evenly across the bottom of the grill, creating one large, hot surface. This setup is ideal for recipes that call for short and hot cook times, such as grilling hot dogs, burgers, fish, moderate-size steaks and chops, and deep-frying.

Indirect-Heat Setup

For an **indirect-heat setup**, the coals are positioned only on one side of the grill, creating a two-zone heating surface. This arrangement offers the most control and flexibility because it allows you to sear foods on the hot side and then slide them (or the pan) over to the unheated—what we call the "hold side"—for more moderate cooking temperatures. For "high heat" cooking, place the food or skillet directly over the coals. For "low heat" cooking, slide the food or pan over to the unheated side. For "medium heat" aim for somewhere in the middle.

There are times when I want high heat for a little longer than just the few minutes it takes to sear a burger or steak. For instance, when you need to bring a pot of water up to boil and then cook pasta, which takes 8 to 12 minutes, depending on the shape. In those cases, the indirect-heat setup tends to work best because you have all the coals concentrated in a smaller area, which gets hotter than if the same amount of coals were spread out across the entire bottom of the grill.

Specialized Grilling Methods

For recipes like braises and slow-smoked meats that require extra-long, moderate-heat cook times (two or more hours), the standard indirect-heat method might fall a little short. That's because the typical chimney starter full of briquettes, when mounded into a single pile on one side of the grill, burns hot and fast, lasting anywhere between 45 and 90 minutes after the initial 15- to 20-minute preheating time. Two big "tricks of the trade" to lengthen cook times are the snake and minion methods, which produce hours of moderate heat. Both techniques accomplish the same thing, but which one you decide to use will depend on your grill equipment.

The Snake Method

For those times when you need a really long-lasting, moderate heat, such as when braising a large chuck roast for Birria-Style Beef Tacos (page 165) or smoking a pork belly (page 155), we could go with the indirect-heat setup, but this is where the "snake method" really shines. The setup involves stacking three to five unlit briquettes in a snake pattern around the perimeter of the grill. One end is ignited, creating a slow, steady heating source as the coals ignite and burn in steady succession. To maintain consistent temperatures, adjust the lower vents until the desired temps are achieved. By placing wood chips or chunks on top of the unlit coals at regular intervals, you can generate flavorful smoke throughout the entire process. This method of cooking can provide up to 12 hours or more of low, steady heat in a **standard kettle-style grill**.

The Minion Method

This method accomplishes the same thing as the snake method—a long, steady, moderate cook—but does so in a slightly different way. It starts by dumping a large quantity of unlit briquettes into the base of the grill and then adding a few hot coals right on top. The lit coals steadily ignite the unlit briquettes beneath them, producing a steady supply of moderate heat. To maintain consistent temperatures, adjust the lower vents until the desired temps are achieved. Again, wood chips can be added to the pile to introduce smoke. This method of cooking can provide up to 12 hours or more of low, steady heat in grills with a smaller diameter, such as **drum, barrel, egg, and kamado grills.**

You don't need a fancy grill to cook amazing food outside!

Replenishing Briquettes

Sometimes you are cooking something for a while, and you need to add more charcoal to the grill. For extra-long cooks like when you're cooking Tomato Tart Tatin (page 25), Braised Lamb Shanks (page 190), and the chili sauce for Coney Dogs (page 141), that might be as simple as topping off the pile of hot coals with some unlit briquettes, which will be ignited (over time) by the others. When I have a nice, hot cook going and I want to keep it that way (without waiting for new briquettes to catch), I will start more briquettes in the chimney and carefully add them to the hot coals in the grill when they are ash-covered and hot.

Getting Started

The best tool for getting your standard direct-heat and indirect-heat setups going is the chimney starter. These bread-loaf-size metal cylinders are filled with unlit briquettes, ignited from below using a lighter and some wadded-up paper (I like to dip mine in leftover bacon or beef fat), and set aside for 15 to 20 minutes to preheat. I usually rest mine on the grill grate while the briquettes are preheating. When almost all of the briquettes are covered in ash and white-hot, the coals are carefully poured into the bottom of the grill.

With the snake and minion methods, the briquettes are arranged in the grill unlit, so no chimney is needed. In those instances, after creating the snake or mound, I light a few coals (either on one end of the snake or the top of the pile with the minion) with a wadded-up piece of paper or chemical-free sawdust starter.

"Smoked" Foods

I absolutely love making real barbecue. In my cookbook *Playing with Fire*, I shared dozens of my favorite recipes for foods like pork belly, pastrami, brisket, and beef ribs that require hours in a real wood-fired smoker. For this book, I wanted to show that pretty much any food can be cooked on a standard kettle-style grill—including smoked items like pork belly. But this is not a barbecue book per se; it's a grilling book. So for most foods I rely on the natural smoke from standard (but chemical- and additive-free) charcoal to add that gentle kiss of smoke. When I want to impart a more prominent degree of smoke flavor—such as in recipes like Smoked Trout (page 116), Pastrami-Smoked Pork Belly (page 155), and Fettuccine with Smoked Tomato Sauce (page 156)— I will add wood chunks. My go-to woods are mild-scented fruitwoods like apple and cherry. I don't soak them with water first, and I only add a handful or two in the beginning of the cook. Just toss the wood on top of the hot coals or, in the case of the snake and minion methods, somewhere in the pile of unlit briquettes.

When I call for salt, I'm using Diamond Crystal kosher salt. If you're using Morton, reduce the quantity called for by half.

Grill Guide

Some grill setups work best for some foods but not others. In other cases, as with thicker burgers and midsize steaks, a home cook can achieve great results using a choice of setups. For example, if I need to cook a large number of burgers, I will go with the high/direct setup because it gives me the largest surface area for cooking. If I had a smaller quantity of foods that might benefit from some indirect cooking after the initial sear, I would go with the high/hold setup. For very long, moderate cooks, the snake and minion are great because they do not require any replenishing of charcoals. The only time you likely will need to replenish coals is for longer cooks (braises, smoking) when neither the snake nor minion is employed.

	DIRECT-HEAT	INDIRECT-HEAT	SNAKE/MINION	REPLENISH BRIQUETTES
Burgers, dogs	X	X		
Fish fillets, thin	X			
Steaks, thin (½-inch to ¾-inch)	X	X		
Steaks, thick (1½-inch +)		X		
Vegetables, long cooking (broccoli, parsnips, carrots)		X		
Vegetables, quick cooking (asparagus, radicchio, shishito peppers)	X			
Boiling water/pasta	X			X
Pan-searing	X			
Deep-frying		X		
Roasts and tough cuts for braising (birria, pork belly)		X	X	X
Cookies, cakes, and pies		X	X	X

Controlling the Grill Temperature

The vents on the bottom of the grill let in air, which fuels the coals. The more oxygen the vents let in, the hotter the coals will burn, and the higher the temps will climb. Likewise, if you partially close the vents to curb air intake, you'll reduce the temperature, too. With practice, you'll be able to reach and maintain the temperatures the recipes require. To obtain and maintain consistent temperatures, it's important to leave the grill cover on and the top vent all the way open.

Bottom Vents Fully Open:

450° to 600°F

All equipment, charcoal, and setups are different, but generally speaking, you can reach high heat (450° to 600°F) when the lower vents are fully open.

Bottom Vents 75% Open:

375° to 425°F

By trimming the vents down to 75 percent open, you can bring the temperature inside the grill down to medium-high heat of 375° to 425°F.

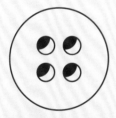

Bottom Vents 50% Open:

300° to 375°F

When the vents are open halfway, expect to see temperatures in the medium range of 300° to 375°F.

Bottom Vents 25% Open:

250° to 300°F

To achieve and maintain temperatures low enough for smoking or braising meats you want the vents open only 25 percent for a low heat of 250° to 300°F.

1

To Start

There are occasions when it makes sense for the entire meal to land on the table at the same time, but those are the exception rather than the rule at our house. More often than not, meals—big, small, just us, or with others—kick off with a snack, starter, or salad. Not only do these dishes offer hungry diners something to dig into right away, but they also buy the cook some much-needed time in the outdoor kitchen. Trust me: If you put out a bowl of Chunky, Spicy Parmesan Dip (page 57) and some crusty, grilled bread, you won't hear a peep out of your guests until it's gone!

In this chapter you'll find light and elegant no-cook salads like Shaved Carrots with Yogurt Dressing (page 32) and a Strawberry and Mint Salad (page 27), as well as fun snacky foods like Grilled Halloumi and Watermelon Kebabs (page 21) and, my personal fave, Fried Clams with Tartar Dipping Sauce (page 49). Many of these recipes can be made hours, or even days, ahead of time, while others require a little hands-on action to prepare. But the beauty of this cookbook is that regardless of the recipe, you will be outside with your guests rather than cooped up alone in a hot kitchen!

Grilled Halloumi and Watermelon Kebabs

Serves 4

1 (8-ounce) package
  Halloumi cheese, cut into
  eight 1-inch cubes
2 cups cubed watermelon
4 (6-inch) skewers, soaked
  in water for at least
  30 minutes if using wood
Extra-virgin olive oil, for
  drizzling
Kosher salt and freshly
  ground black pepper
Hot honey, for serving
¼ cup finely chopped fresh
  mint, for garnish

My mom used to make versions of this in the summer when watermelon was at its peak of ripeness. Like the popular feta-watermelon salad, this one counters the sweetness of the melon with the salty punch of cheese. But I manage to pack in a ton more flavor and texture by using Halloumi, a nonmelting cheese that's *made* for the grill. The pairing of warm, smoky, chewy, salty cheese and juicy-sweet watermelon is going to blow you—and your guests—away!

1. Prepare and preheat a charcoal grill for direct cooking.

2. Thread alternating cubes of Halloumi and watermelon onto each of the 4 skewers, grouping them near the top so that the tip is covered by the food, but leaving space to grab the skewer at the bottom.

3. Drizzle the skewers on all sides with olive oil, season with a pinch of salt and twist of pepper, place on the grill, and cook until nicely charred, about 1 minute per side.

4. Transfer the skewers to a platter, drizzle with hot honey to taste, garnish with the mint, and serve.

Smoked and Steamed Artichokes

Serves 4

Artichokes

½ lemon
½ cup dry white wine
Small bunch of fresh dill
2 garlic cloves, smashed
   and peeled
2 large globe artichokes

Tarragon Aioli

½ cup mayonnaise
3 tablespoons extra-virgin
   olive oil
Grated zest and juice of
   ½ lemon
2 teaspoons finely chopped
   fresh tarragon
1 garlic clove, grated
Kosher salt and freshly
   ground black pepper

Steamed artichokes bring me so much joy. I just love plucking off the fat petals, dragging them through some creamy sauce, and squeezing the earthy flesh between my teeth and into my mouth. We manage to improve on the classic dish by giving the artichokes some time to roast over coals, which brings some smoky goodness to the party, before poaching them in a dill-scented bath. We marry those flavors with a zippy tarragon-flavored aioli. If you're one of those people who don't love tarragon, go ahead and swap in basil, dill, or even cilantro.

1. Prepare and preheat a charcoal grill for indirect cooking, with one hot side and one hold (unheated) side.

2. Prepare the artichokes: Squeeze the lemon into 4 cups water. In a large soup pot, combine the lemon water, wine, dill, and garlic. Set the pot on the hot side of the grill and bring to a gentle boil.

3. Meanwhile, with a sharp knife, cut off the top 1 inch of the artichokes. Using shears, trim the tips off each outer leaf. Use a vegetable peeler to remove the woody exterior on the stems. Remove all but 1 inch of the stems. Prick the end of the stems with a fork a few times. Place the artichokes on the hold side of the grill while the water comes to a boil.

4. When the water comes to a gentle boil, add the artichokes stem-side up, cover the pot, and cook until easily pierced by a fork, about 30 minutes.

5. Meanwhile, make the tarragon aioli: In a medium bowl, whisk together the mayonnaise, olive oil, lemon zest, lemon juice, tarragon, and garlic. Season with a pinch of salt and twist of pepper.

6. Transfer the artichokes to a platter and serve with aioli on the side.

Tomato Tart Tatin

Serves 6

2 pounds plum tomatoes, halved lengthwise and cored

Kosher salt and freshly ground black pepper

3 tablespoons sugar

3 tablespoons red wine vinegar

2 medium yellow onions, halved and thinly sliced (about 2 cups)

2 garlic cloves, grated

2 tablespoons finely chopped fresh flat-leaf parsley

1 tablespoon fresh thyme leaves

¼ cup extra-virgin olive oil

1 tablespoon unsalted butter

1 (10 × 15-inch) sheet frozen puff pastry, thawed

Flaky sea salt, for serving

Sprig of fresh basil, for serving

Like many vegetables, tomatoes are transformed when roasted, with the heat of the grill accentuating the sweetness of summer's most popular garden item. This dish is a savory riff on the classic dessert, apple tarte Tatin. The tomatoes cook slowly on a bed of onions and herbs, which infuses them with so much flavor. I build this dish upside down in the pan, so that when it's inverted onto a platter, the pastry is on the bottom and the gorgeous tomatoes are on top. Make sure that the grill is well preheated—we call for around 325°F—which ensures a proper puff and golden-brown color. You could serve it as a starter along with some crusty bread or even paired with a salad for a light lunch.

1. Prepare and preheat a charcoal grill for indirect cooking, with one hot side and one hold (unheated) side. Adjust the grill vents to maintain a temperature of 300° to 375°F (see Controlling the Grill Temperature, page 17).

2. Season the cut sides of the tomatoes with a pinch of kosher salt and a couple twists of pepper and set aside.

3. Set a large enameled cast-iron pan on the hot side of the grill, add the sugar, and shake it out into an even layer. Cook, without stirring, until the sugar melts and caramelizes, about 10 minutes. Add the vinegar to deglaze the pan, followed by the onions, garlic, parsley, and thyme. Cook, stirring occasionally, until reduced to a thick syrup, about 5 minutes. Stir in the olive oil.

4. Remove the pan from the heat and add the tomatoes cut-side down. Place the pan on the hold side of the grill, cover the grill, and cook until the tomatoes are very soft and the skins wrinkly, about 2 hours. Top off the charcoal as needed (see Replenishing Briquettes, page 15). Carefully remove and discard the tomato skins (they should slip right off).

5. When the tomatoes are done, place a second large enameled cast-iron pan over the hot side of the grill and add the butter. Swirl the pan to evenly distribute the butter. Remove both pans from the heat. Leaving as much liquid, onions, and herbs in the first pan as possible, transfer the baked tomatoes to the buttered skillet, arranging them cut-side up. Arrange the cooked onions and herbs from the first pan in an even layer on top of the tomatoes.

recipe continues

6. Using shears, trim off about an inch from each corner of the puff pastry to make a rough round. It doesn't have to be perfect. Carefully place the pastry on top of the tomatoes (not the rim of the skillet). Using a sharp knife, cut three small slits into the center of the pastry to vent steam.

7. Place the pan on the hold side of the grill and cover the grill. Adjust the grill vents to maintain a temperature of 425°F (see Controlling the Grill Temperature, page 17). Bake until the pastry is slightly puffed and golden brown, about 25 minutes. Remove from the heat and allow to cool for 3 minutes.

8. Carefully invert the tart onto a plate so that the pastry is now on the bottom and the tomatoes are on top. Sprinkle with flaky salt, garnish with a sprig of fresh basil, and serve.

Strawberry and Mint Salad

Serves 4

3 tablespoons red wine vinegar

1 tablespoon Dijon mustard

1 tablespoon raw honey

½ cup extra-virgin olive oil

Kosher salt and freshly ground black pepper

4 cups quartered hulled strawberries

4 cups loosely packed arugula

½ cup finely chopped fresh mint

1 cup slivered toasted almonds

6 ounces crumbled goat cheese (about 1 cup)

This might be the perfect summer salad! Strawberry and mint is one of those magical food pairings that makes your taste buds go crazy. We boost the sweetness with a kiss of honey in the vinaigrette and garnish it with creamy goat cheese and crunchy toasted almonds. If you're making Spatchcock Chicken (page 147)—or any grilled meat—this is your side dish!

1. In a medium bowl, whisk together the vinegar, mustard, honey, and olive oil. Season with a pinch of salt and twist of pepper. Add the strawberries, arugula, mint, and half the toasted almonds and toss to combine.

2. Transfer the salad to a platter, top with the goat cheese and remaining almonds, and serve.

Avocado, Orange, and Jicama Salad

Serves 4

½ cup extra-virgin olive oil

¼ cup sherry vinegar

2 teaspoons raw honey

Kosher salt and freshly ground black pepper

1 small jicama, peeled and diced (about 2 cups)

4 navel oranges, peeled and divided into segments

1 jalapeño, seeded and minced

¼ cup roughly chopped fresh cilantro

4 avocados, sliced

Flaky sea salt, for serving

If you love avocado but can't stand to look at another slice of "avo toast," add this dish to your repertoire. It's a medley of tropical flavors, textures, and colors that brightens any meal. For a super-elegant presentation, I like to arrange the avocado slices in an overlapping shingle pattern on a platter before topping it with the orange and jicama salad. If there was ever a lesson in not judging a book by its cover, it's the odd-looking jicama. Beneath that drab exterior is a unique and crunchy veggie that pairs well with almost everything.

1. In a medium bowl, whisk together the olive oil, vinegar, and honey. Season with a pinch of kosher salt and twist of pepper. Add the jicama, oranges, jalapeño, and cilantro and toss to combine.

2. Arrange the avocado slices in an overlapping pattern on a platter. Season with flaky sea salt and a twist of black pepper. Top with the orange and jicama salad and serve.

Crispy Pita Salad

Serves 4

¼ cup red wine vinegar
1 garlic clove, grated
1 teaspoon finely chopped
  fresh oregano
½ cup extra-virgin olive oil
Kosher salt and freshly
  ground black pepper
1 (15-ounce) can chickpeas,
  drained and rinsed
2 medium cucumbers, diced
  (about 2 cups)
2 beefsteak tomatoes, diced
2 heads romaine lettuce,
  cored and thinly sliced
2 heads radicchio, cored
  and thinly sliced
1 cup crumbled Greek feta
  cheese
4 cups pita chips

If you've ever had panzanella, the famous Tuscan salad that combines stale bread and summer-ripe veggies, then you have an idea where I'm going with this. In place of the standard Italian bread, I call for crispy-crunchy store-bought pita chips. But like the classic it's modeled after, this recipe is a great way to use up stale pita. Or tear some fresh pita into pieces, toss them in some olive oil and seasonings, and grill them until lightly charred and crisp! Thrifty and delicious!

In a medium bowl, whisk together the vinegar, garlic, oregano, and olive oil. Season with a pinch of salt and twist of pepper. Add the chickpeas, cucumbers, tomatoes, romaine, radicchio, feta, and pita chips and toss to combine. Garnish with a few more twists of black pepper and serve.

Shaved Carrots
with Yogurt Dressing

Serves 4

½ cup whole-milk Greek
yogurt
¼ cup extra-virgin olive oil
Grated zest of 1 lemon
Juice of 2 lemons
2 tablespoons raw honey
1 garlic clove, minced
1 teaspoon Urfa pepper,
Aleppo pepper, or red
pepper flakes
½ teaspoon ground cumin
½ teaspoon ground
coriander
Kosher salt and freshly
ground black pepper
4 medium carrots, shaved
with a vegetable peeler
(about 4 cups)
1 cup torn fresh mint leaves
1 cup toasted pistachios

It's amazing how the simple act of shaving a vegetable—as opposed to chopping or slicing it—can change the whole dynamic of a dish. I like to shave radishes, beets, Brussels sprouts, and even asparagus with a mandoline or good vegetable peeler for use in uncooked applications like salads. Here, carrot ribbons, crunchy pistachios, and heaps of fresh mint are tossed together in a refreshing cumin and coriander-spiced dressing. I've been loving Urfa pepper lately, a smoky-sweet chile powder, and add it to the dressing, too, but you can substitute Aleppo or plain red pepper flakes. To supercharge this dish, toast the spices in a hot, dry skillet until they become fragrant. It's worth the added effort!

In a medium bowl, whisk together the yogurt, olive oil, lemon zest, lemon juice, honey, garlic, Urfa pepper, cumin, and coriander. Season with a pinch of salt and twist of black pepper. Add the carrots, mint, and pistachios, toss to combine, and serve.

Charred Broccoli Salad

Serves 4

Buttermilk Dressing

1 cup buttermilk
½ cup sour cream
¼ cup apple cider vinegar
2 tablespoons light brown
    sugar
2 tablespoons finely
    chopped fresh dill
1 tablespoon brown
    ballpark-style mustard
⅛ teaspoon freshly grated
    nutmeg
Kosher salt and freshly
    ground black pepper

Salad

2 medium heads broccoli
Extra-virgin olive oil, for
    drizzling
Kosher salt and freshly
    ground black pepper
½ cup roughly chopped
    salted roasted peanuts
½ cup dried cherries
2 scallions, white and light-
    green parts only, thinly
    sliced (about ¼ cup)

If you have someone in the family who opposes all things broccoli, fire up this amazing recipe. In place of the typical waterlogged steamed broccoli buried beneath a gloopy cheese sauce, I start with charred but crisp-tender broccoli. After coming off the grill, it's drizzled with tangy buttermilk dressing and garnished with crunchy peanuts and tart cherries. If you want to make the broccoli easier to grill, cut the heads into four large sections (okay, you can call them trees) instead of small florets. It all depends on your grill and grate setup.

1. Prepare and preheat a charcoal grill for indirect cooking, with one hot side and one hold (unheated) side.

2. Make the buttermilk dressing: In a medium bowl, whisk together the buttermilk, sour cream, vinegar, brown sugar, dill, mustard, and nutmeg. Season with a pinch of salt and twist of pepper. Cover and refrigerate until needed.

3. Prepare the salad: Cut the broccoli into small florets.

4. Drizzle the broccoli on all sides with olive oil and season with a few pinches of salt and twists of black pepper. Put the broccoli on the hot side of the grill and cook, without moving, until nicely charred on all sides, about 2 minutes per side. Move the broccoli to the hold side of the grill, cover, and cook until easily pierced by a fork, about 5 minutes.

5. Transfer the broccoli to a platter, drizzle with the buttermilk dressing, garnish with the peanuts, cherries, and scallions, and serve.

Feta Waffles
with Fresh Tomato Salsa

Makes 4 waffles

Tomato Salsa

½ cup extra-virgin olive oil
½ cup pitted kalamata olives
2 tablespoons finely chopped fresh flat-leaf parsley
1 tablespoon finely chopped fresh oregano
2 garlic cloves, minced
Grated zest of 1 lemon
2 cups halved yellow and red cherry tomatoes
Kosher salt and freshly ground black pepper

Waffles

Cooking spray
1 cup all-purpose flour
½ cup whole milk
1 large egg
1 teaspoon baking powder
2 tablespoons unsalted butter, melted
1 (8-ounce) block Greek feta cheese, crumbled

A waffle iron is one of those kitchen gadgets that is indispensable for making waffles (obviously). But don't just bust it out of the kitchen cupboard for those breakfast staples when there is so much more you can do with it. Here I press and cook feta-enriched waffles until they are golden brown and crisp and then serve them with an herby tomato salsa. Talk about a flavor explosion! Serve these treats at a backyard barbecue and you'll be a hero. (I highly recommend waffling leftover mashed potatoes, too, by the way!)

1. Make the tomato salsa: In a blender or food processor, combine the olive oil, olives, parsley, oregano, garlic, and lemon zest and pulse until coarsely chopped. Transfer to a large bowl and fold in the tomatoes. Season the salsa with salt and pepper.

2. Make the waffles: Preheat a waffle iron to high. Grease the top and bottom plates with cooking spray.

3. In a large bowl, add the flour, milk, egg, baking powder, and melted butter and whisk to combine. Fold in the feta.

4. Working in batches, put the batter in the center of the waffle iron, press down the lid, and cook until golden brown and crisp, about 5 minutes.

5. Carefully transfer the waffles to a cutting board and cut into squares or wedges. Top with the tomato salsa and serve.

Tomato and Anchovy Bread

Serves 4

4 slices (1-inch-thick) rustic bread

4 tablespoons extra-virgin olive oil

Kosher salt and freshly ground black pepper

2 garlic cloves, peeled but whole

2 large very ripe tomatoes, halved

12 oil-packed whole white anchovies

2 tablespoons roughly chopped fresh flat-leaf parsley

Flaky sea salt, for serving

In terms of flavor vs. ease of assembly, it's tough to top these toasts (say that five times fast!). It's no secret that I love anchovies because they pack so much goodness into a small (and cheap and nonperishable) package. In *Simply Symon Suppers* I included a version of anchovy toast that I make all summer long. This recipe marries that preparation with the classic Spanish *pan con tomate*, or tomato bread, by adding a layer of sweet, juicy tomato. By using good-quality white anchovies—which are vinegar-cured as opposed to salt-cured—we end up with a brighter but milder flavor profile. Serve this as a snack or a starter or top it with mozzarella or burrata and call it a salad or side dish.

1. Prepare and preheat a charcoal grill for indirect cooking, with one hot side and one hold (unheated) side.

2. Brush both sides of the bread slices with the olive oil, season with a few pinches of kosher salt and twists of pepper, and place on the hot side of the grill. Cook until slightly charred and toasted on both sides, about 30 seconds per side.

3. While the bread is still warm, rub each slice with the garlic cloves until aromatic. Rub and press the cut tomatoes onto the bread so that some of the flesh and juice transfers to the bread, leaving the skin behind. Discard the skins.

4. Top each toast with 3 anchovies, garnish with parsley and flaky sea salt, and serve.

Savory Herb and Parmesan Rolls

Makes 6 rolls

Dough

1 cup lukewarm whole milk (about 110°F)

1 teaspoon active dry yeast

1 teaspoon plus 2 tablespoons sugar

2 tablespoons unsalted butter

2 cups bread flour, plus more for rolling

¼ teaspoon kosher salt

1 large egg yolk

Olive oil or cooking spray, for greasing

Filling

1 cup finely grated parmesan cheese

4 scallions, white and light-green parts only, thinly sliced (about ½ cup)

½ cup finely chopped fresh flat-leaf parsley

4 tablespoons (½ stick) unsalted butter, at room temperature

1 garlic clove, minced

Kosher salt and freshly ground black pepper

Assembly and Serving

1 garlic clove, peeled but whole

2 tablespoons unsalted butter

Hot honey

Freshly grated parmesan cheese

Flaky sea salt

I'm not going to lie: This recipe is a lot more involved than your basic garlic bread. But the results are also a million times better than plain-old garlic bread, so it's worth it! Imagine a savory, sinful version of a cinnamon roll, all pillowy and lush, but with butter, garlic, scallions, and cheese. There's no need to turn on an oven and heat up the whole kitchen when a grill can do the same work and produce equally delicious results! You can omit the hot honey if you're not a fan, but do not skip the crunchy sea salt. I think it takes the rolls to a whole different level.

1. Prepare and preheat a charcoal grill for indirect cooking, with one hot side and one hold (unheated) side.

2. Make the dough: In a stand mixer fitted with the dough hook, combine the milk, yeast, and 1 teaspoon of the sugar and let sit until very foamy, about 10 minutes.

3. Meanwhile, set a small saucepan on the hold (unheated) side of the grill, add the butter, and cook, stirring, until the butter begins to brown and smell nutty, about 5 minutes. Be careful not to let the butter burn. Remove from the heat to cool.

4. In a medium bowl, whisk together the flour, the remaining 2 tablespoons sugar, and the salt.

5. Add the brown butter, egg yolk, and flour mixture to the yeast mixture and blend on medium until it begins to pull away from the bowl, about 5 minutes. Continue blending on medium until the dough is shiny and elastic, about 5 minutes. Turn the dough out into a lightly greased bowl, turn the dough to coat all sides, cover with plastic wrap, and let rise until doubled in size, about 1 hour.

6. Meanwhile, make the filling: In a large bowl, stir together the parmesan, scallions, parsley, butter, and garlic until thoroughly combined. Season liberally with pinches of salt and twists of pepper.

7. Assemble the rolls: Rub the bottom and sides of a 10-inch cast-iron skillet with the garlic, place it on the hold side of the grill, and add the butter. When the butter has melted, swirl the pan to completely coat the bottom and sides. Remove from the heat.

recipe continues

8. Turn the dough out onto a lightly floured surface. Use a rolling pin to roll out the dough to a 5 × 15-inch rectangle about ¼ inch thick. With a long side facing you, spread the filling evenly over the dough, taking it all the way to the edges but leaving a ½-inch border on the side farthest from you. Working on the side nearest to you, roll the dough into a tight roll, pinching the seam closed. Slice into 6 equal rounds and place cut-side down in the buttered skillet, leaving some space in between. Cover with plastic wrap and let rise at room temperature until almost doubled in size, about 30 minutes.

9. Discard the plastic wrap and cover the skillet with a lid. Place the skillet on the hold side of the grill and cook at 325°F until the rolls are golden brown, about 25 minutes.

10. Turn the rolls out onto a plate, drizzle with hot honey to taste, sprinkle with parmesan and flaky salt, and serve.

Spicy Cucumber Salad

Serves 4

2 cucumbers, quartered
  lengthwise and cut into
  2-inch pieces (about
  4 cups)
1 small red onion, halved
  and thinly sliced (about
  ½ cup)
Kosher salt
½ cup sour cream
⅓ cup finely chopped fresh
  dill
2 tablespoons white wine
  vinegar
1 tablespoon extra-virgin
  olive oil
2 teaspoons hot sauce
1 garlic clove, grated
Freshly ground black pepper

I've included more than a few cucumber salad recipes in my cookbooks over the years, including the perfect (if I do say so myself!) version in *Playing with Fire.* Like that one, this preparation blends crunchy cukes and red onions with creamy sour cream, but here we kick up the heat with some hot sauce and punch up the flavor with fresh garlic. Also, instead of the typical thin-sliced cucumbers, we opt for a more rustic chunky cut. Serve this refreshing side dish with absolutely any grilled fish, meat, or poultry dish.

1. Place the cucumbers and onion in a large bowl and sprinkle liberally with salt. Let stand while you make the vinaigrette.

2. In a medium bowl, whisk together the sour cream, dill, vinegar, olive oil, hot sauce, and garlic. Season with a pinch of salt and twist of pepper. Pour the dressing over the cucumber and onion, toss to combine, and serve.

Avocado and Cucumber Salad

Serves 4

¼ cup extra-virgin olive oil
Grated zest of 1 lime
Juice of 2 limes
1 tablespoon raw honey
Kosher salt and freshly
  ground black pepper
2 avocados, large diced
1 medium cucumber, large
  diced (about 2 cups)
1 medium red onion, halved
  and thinly sliced (about
  1 cup)
1 small jalapeño, seeded
  and minced
1 cup fresh cilantro leaves
3 tablespoons toasted
  sesame seeds

Liz and I are always looking for new ways to enjoy avocados because they are so healthy and delicious. It takes a little "avocado management" to ensure that there's always a couple ripe ones at the ready. When there are, we make nutrient-rich salads like this one. Serve it on its own or as a side dish with grilled fish. If you want to add a different dimension to this salad, try grilling avocado halves—which gives them a smoky essence and creamy texture—prior to chopping and adding them to the rest of the ingredients.

In a medium bowl, whisk together the olive oil, lime zest, lime juice, and honey. Season with a pinch of salt and twist of pepper. Add the avocado, cucumber, onion, jalapeño, cilantro, and sesame seeds. Gently toss to combine and serve.

Grill-Roasted Parsnips
with Chestnut Honey Brown Butter

Serves 4

4 tablespoons (½ stick) unsalted butter

2 tablespoons chestnut honey

Grated zest and juice of 1 orange

Kosher salt and freshly ground black pepper

⅓ cup cubed pancetta

4 large parsnips, scrubbed and halved lengthwise

2 tablespoons extra-virgin olive oil

3 cups watercress, loosely packed

Chestnut honey, which is made by bees that gather nectar from flowering chestnut trees, is like honey on steroids. Dark in color and robust in flavor, this distinctive condiment is like a secret weapon in your grilling arsenal. When combined with brown butter, as we do here, you wind up with a truly seductive glaze that improves everything it graces. Parsnips, like most vegetables, soften and sweeten on the grill. We finish them with that nutty, fruity glaze and pair them with fresh and peppery watercress.

1. Prepare and preheat a charcoal grill for indirect cooking, with one hot side and one hold (unheated) side.

2. Set a small saucepan on the hot side of the grill and add the butter. Cook, stirring frequently, until the butter begins to brown and smell nutty, about 5 minutes. Be careful not to let the butter burn. Remove from the heat. Whisk in the honey, orange zest, and orange juice and season with a pinch of salt and twist of pepper.

3. Set a cast-iron skillet on the hot side of the grill. Add the pancetta and cook, stirring frequently, until it begins to brown, about 5 minutes. Drizzle the parsnips with olive oil and season both sides with salt and black pepper. Add the parsnips to the pan with the pancetta, slide the pan to the hold side of the grill, cover the grill, and cook for 20 minutes.

4. Transfer the parsnips to a platter, spoon on the brown butter sauce, top with the watercress, and serve.

Grilled Shishito Peppers
with Burrata
Serves 4

24 shishito peppers,
    stemmed
1 small red onion, quartered
7 tablespoons extra-virgin
    olive oil
Kosher salt and freshly
    ground black pepper
4 slices (¾-inch-thick) rustic
    bread
2 tablespoons sherry
    vinegar
2 tablespoons hot honey
2 anchovy fillets, finely
    chopped
1 garlic clove, minced
1 cup torn fresh mint leaves
2 (4-ounce) balls burrata

You typically see burrata paired with tomatoes, but I enjoy it with the sometimes-hot, sometimes-not shishito pepper. Even without the burrata, this salad of warm, grilled chile peppers in a sweet, salty, and tangy dressing is a banger. Toss in some luscious burrata and crusty bread (or better yet, grilled bread) for scooping and it turns into a sharable appetizer that people will talk about for days. While I rarely find a truly blistering-hot shishito, if you can't take the risk of biting into a scorcher, you can substitute with those adorable baby bell peppers—red, yellow, orange!—instead.

1. Prepare and preheat a charcoal grill for direct cooking.

2. In a large bowl, toss together the peppers, onion, and 1 tablespoon of the olive oil to coat. Season with a pinch of salt and twist of pepper.

3. Set a large perforated pan on the grill. Add the pepper/onion mixture and cook, stirring occasionally, until lightly charred, about 3 minutes.

4. Meanwhile, brush both sides of the bread slices with 2 tablespoons of the olive oil, season with salt and pepper, and place on the grill. Cook until slightly charred and toasted on both sides, about 30 seconds per side.

5. In a medium bowl, whisk together the vinegar, hot honey, anchovies, garlic, and remaining 4 tablespoons olive oil. Season with a pinch of salt and twist of pepper. Add the cooked peppers and onions and toss to coat. Add the mint and toss again.

6. Place the burrata on a platter, cut each ball in half, top with the pepper mixture, and serve with the grilled bread.

Fried Clams
with Tartar Dipping Sauce
Serves 4

Tartar Sauce
1 cup creamy horseradish
   sauce
½ medium red onion, grated
   on the large holes of a
   box grater (about ½ cup)
¼ cup sweet relish
¼ cup finely chopped
   fresh dill
Juice of 1 lemon
Hot sauce
Kosher salt and freshly
   ground black pepper

Fried Clams
1 (12-ounce) can
   evaporated milk
1 tablespoon hot sauce, or
   to taste
24 freshly shucked clams,
   such as Ipswich clams
Neutral oil, for deep-frying
1 cup corn flour
1 teaspoon garlic powder
1 teaspoon onion powder
Kosher salt and freshly
   ground black pepper
1 lemon, cut into wedges,
   for serving

The first time I had this style of clams was at Woodman's of
Essex, located about an hour north of Boston. That restaurant is
famous for being the first to offer fried clams, which it did more
than one hundred years ago. When I visited, everyone around
me was eating lobster, but I couldn't stop eating the fried clams.
The key is to start with whole-belly soft-shell clams, often called
steamers, Ipswich clams, or Essex clams. They aren't very easy
to find outside of the Northeast because their brittle shells make
them difficult to ship. When properly cooked, they are lightly
golden brown, plump, briny, and sweet. I could literally eat them
every day.

1. Make the tartar sauce: In a medium bowl, whisk together the
   horseradish sauce, onion, relish, dill, lemon juice, and hot sauce
   to taste. Season with a pinch of salt and a twist of black pepper.
   Cover and refrigerate until needed.

2. Make the fried clams: In a medium bowl, whisk together the
   evaporated milk and hot sauce. Add the clams and gently stir to
   coat. Cover and refrigerate for 1 hour.

3. Prepare and preheat a charcoal grill for direct cooking.

4. Set a deep heavy-bottomed pot on the grill. Add 4 inches of oil
   and heat to 350°F. Set a wire rack over a sheet pan lined with
   paper towels.

5. In a shallow bowl, whisk together the corn flour, garlic powder,
   and onion powder. Season with a pinch of salt and a twist of
   black pepper.

6. Remove the clams from the marinade, allowing most of the
   marinade to drip off. Add the clams to the seasoned corn flour
   mixture and toss to fully coat. Working in two batches to not
   crowd the pan, fry the clams until golden brown, stirring once,
   about 2 minutes. Use a slotted spoon to transfer the clams to the
   rack and season with a pinch of salt.

7. Serve immediately with tartar sauce and lemon wedges on the side.

Jerusalem Artichoke Puree
with Ground Lamb and Mint

Serves 4

2 pounds Jerusalem
  artichokes, peeled
Grated zest and juice
  of 1 lemon
Kosher salt
6 tablespoons extra-virgin
  olive oil
1 pound ground lamb
2 garlic cloves, minced
1 teaspoon sweet paprika
½ teaspoon ground
  coriander
½ teaspoon ground cumin
¼ teaspoon ground
  cinnamon
3 tablespoons finely
  chopped fresh flat-leaf
  parsley
3 tablespoons finely
  chopped fresh mint
4 tablespoons (½ stick)
  unsalted butter
Freshly ground black pepper
1 lemon, cut into 8 wedges

When it comes to underrated—or simply ignored—ingredients, Jerusalem artichokes are near the top of the list. Sometimes called sunchokes, this curious vegetable is the tuberous root of a certain type of sunflower (sunchokes . . . get it?). When cooked, they take on a delightfully earthy-sweet flavor. Here we cook and puree them to use as a base for a spiced ground lamb mixture, in much the same way that hummus might be employed. Serve with lemon and a few glugs of good olive oil.

1. Prepare and preheat a charcoal grill for direct cooking.

2. In a large saucepan, combine the Jerusalem artichokes, lemon juice, and large pinch of salt. Cover with cold water and bring to a boil on the grill. Simmer until easily pierced by a fork, about 40 minutes.

3. Meanwhile, set a large skillet on the grill, add 2 tablespoons of the olive oil, and heat to shimmering. Add the ground lamb, garlic, paprika, coriander, cumin, cinnamon, and a pinch of salt. Cook, stirring with a wooden spoon to break up the meat, until lightly browned, about 5 minutes. Remove the pan from the heat and stir in the lemon zest, parsley, and mint.

4. When the Jerusalem artichokes are tender, use a slotted spoon to transfer them to a blender (discard the water) or use an immersion blender. Add the butter and process until smooth. Season with a pinch of salt and twist of pepper.

5. Transfer the artichoke puree to a platter. Use the back of a large spoon to make a well in the center, add the lamb, garnish with the remaining 4 tablespoons olive oil and the lemon wedges, and serve.

Peaches
with Fresh Mozzarella and Prosciutto

Serves 4

3 peaches, each cut into
8 wedges

1 (8-ounce) ball fresh
mozzarella, thinly sliced

Kosher salt and freshly
ground black pepper

4 ounces very thinly sliced
prosciutto

6 tablespoons smoked maple
syrup or plain maple syrup

¼ cup extra-virgin olive oil

¼ cup jarred pickled
mustard seeds

1 cup fresh basil leaves

If you're on the hunt for an impressive summer appetizer that requires no cooking whatsoever, look no further. Assuming you can find ripe, juicy peaches, the rest of the ingredients are available at most grocery stores. Start with some good-quality thin-sliced prosciutto, add some fresh and milky mozz, and drizzle on some smoky-sweet maple syrup. Even if you don't think you like mustard, pickled mustard seeds add another layer of textural excitement—just pick up a jar from the condiment aisle.

Arrange the peaches on a platter and top with the sliced mozzarella. Season with a few pinches of salt and twists of pepper. Drape the prosciutto slices on the peaches. Drizzle with the maple syrup and olive oil. Scatter the mustard seeds over the top, garnish with the basil, and serve.

Cauliflower "Risotto"

Serves 4

1 medium head cauliflower, cut into chunky florets
2 tablespoons extra-virgin olive oil
1 small yellow onion, roughly chopped (about ½ cup)
1 garlic clove, minced
Kosher salt
½ cup pine nuts
½ cup dry white wine
1 cup vegetable stock
1 cup heavy cream
1 tablespoon chopped fresh thyme
½ teaspoon freshly grated nutmeg
¼ cup freshly grated parmesan cheese
2 tablespoons unsalted butter
2 tablespoons chopped fresh chives
Freshly ground black pepper

I make a killer risotto. The main reason that is true is because I absolutely adore the process, from toasting the rice to patiently adding the warm stock, cup by cup. This "risotto" is not that risotto—not by a long shot. But it is delicious, indulgent, and satisfying in its own way. Oh yeah, and it's ready in less than 15 minutes! Serve it in place of a starch like rice, polenta, or mashed potatoes and pretend it's a healthy vegetable dish.

1. Prepare and preheat a charcoal grill for direct cooking.

2. Grate the florets and tender stems of the cauliflower on the large holes of a box grater.

3. Set a large skillet on the grill. Add the olive oil and heat to shimmering. Add the onion, garlic, and a large pinch of salt. Cook, stirring occasionally, until the vegetables begin to soften, about 2 minutes. Add the grated cauliflower and pine nuts and cook, stirring occasionally, for 2 minutes. Add the wine, bring to a strong simmer, and cook, stirring occasionally, until the wine has reduced by half, about 2 minutes. Add the stock, cream, thyme, and nutmeg and cook, stirring occasionally, until the sauce has been reduced by two-thirds, about 5 minutes.

4. Remove from the heat and stir in the parmesan, butter, and chives. Taste and adjust for seasoning, adding salt and pepper as needed, and serve.

Chunky, Spicy Parmesan Dip

Serves 6

1 pound parmesan cheese, broken into ¼- to ½-inch chunks

2 cups extra-virgin olive oil

¼ cup finely chopped fresh flat-leaf parsley

2 tablespoons dried oregano, preferably Sicilian

1 tablespoon freshly ground black pepper

1 tablespoon red pepper flakes

3 garlic cloves, minced

Grated zest of 2 lemons

Bread, for serving (if you have the grill on for other stuff, grill the bread too!)

When I was a young cook, my friend (and cookbook producer and Cleveland native) Susie Heller introduced me to a dish called "parmigiana glop." It's a very unappetizing name for a very appetizing snack. Essentially, it's a chunky cheese dip that goes great on bread, crackers, or even soft pretzels. From the minute I tasted it all those years ago, I knew that some version of it would be a part of my entertaining repertoire forever. At my restaurant Angeline at the Borgata in Atlantic City, we have a version of this yummy spread that we serve with grilled Italian bread. Use the best-quality parmesan cheese you can find for this.

In a food processor, pulse the parmesan until it has the consistency of coarse crumbs (larger than panko but smaller than a crouton). Transfer to a medium bowl, add the olive oil, parsley, oregano, black pepper, pepper flakes, garlic, and lemon zest and stir to blend. Serve with bread for dipping.

2

Plays Nice with Others

If we were to think of an entire meal as a film, the main dish would be the leading actor and the side dishes would be the supporting cast. If you happen to be a film lover like me, then you know that it's the supporting actors who help move the story along while having that all-important chemistry with the star. That's how I look at side dishes. Rather than just providing filler, these pivotal plates add richness and texture to a meal, elevating the occasion simply by their presence.

I think some home cooks focus too much on the main event when they should be paying *at least equal* attention to the side dishes. I love a great steak, for example, and sometimes I prefer to cut the richness of the dish by pairing it with a side like Grilled Greens with Lime Vinaigrette (page 81) or My Favorite Asparagus (page 77). Other times, I go full-on indulgent by serving it with something like Creamed Leeks with Thyme (page 71) or Duck Fat–Fried Fondant Potatoes (page 78). That's the power of the side dish, to steer a meal in one direction or another.

I think one of the easiest ways for a home cook to up his or her game is by picking the side dishes that will "play nice" with the other dishes on the table. Thanks to the perfect pairing, your guests might not even be fully aware of why they're enjoying themselves so much.

Old Bay Grilled Corn

Serves 4

4 ears corn, shucked
4 cups buttermilk
1 tablespoon Old Bay
seasoning, plus more for
serving
Kosher salt and freshly
ground black pepper

Growing up in Ohio, corn season was a big deal—like football season, but without all the disappointment. From midsummer through fall, our family would find countless ways to enjoy this crop. While I'll always love a briefly boiled ear slathered with butter, more and more I've been turning to the grill for my preps. A short cook on a hot grill prevents overcooking, and I just think everything is better with a nice char. The buttermilk brine in this recipe enhances the caramelization while bringing the seasoning deep into the kernels. I like to sprinkle a little more Old Bay on the corn after it comes off the grill.

1. Place the corn in a 1-gallon zip-top bag. In a medium bowl, whisk together the buttermilk and Old Bay. Season with a pinch of salt and twist of pepper. Pour the marinade over the corn and refrigerate for at least 1 hour and up to 4 hours.

2. Prepare and preheat a charcoal grill for direct cooking.

3. Remove the corn from the buttermilk, allowing the excess marinade to drip off. Place on the grill and cook until nicely charred on all sides, about 2 minutes per side.

4. Season to taste with salt, pepper, and Old Bay and serve.

Grilled Radicchio
with Buttermilk Dressing

Serves 4

Buttermilk Dressing

1 cup buttermilk

½ cup sour cream

¼ cup mayonnaise

¼ cup finely chopped fresh
flat-leaf parsley

¼ cup thinly sliced fresh
basil

2 tablespoons thinly sliced
fresh chives

2 garlic cloves, grated

Kosher salt and freshly
ground black pepper

Grilled Radicchio

2 cups ciabatta bread cubes

3 tablespoons extra-virgin
olive oil, plus more for
drizzling

Kosher salt and freshly
ground black pepper

2 heads radicchio, quartered

Freshly grated parmesan
cheese, for serving

For a while there, grilled Caesar salads were all the rage. The preparation is a fresh way to update a classic, but there are real benefits to it as well. Grilling the greens—typically a head of romaine sliced lengthwise—adds sweetness and texture. But it also looks really cool, and the interplay of warm and cold ingredients adds another layer of interest. That's the idea behind this recipe, where a brief grilling tames the natural bitterness of the radicchio. Toss it with some toasted bread crumbs and creamy buttermilk dressing and you've got another grilled salad winner.

1. Prepare and preheat a charcoal grill for indirect cooking, with one hot side and one hold (unheated) side.

2. Make the buttermilk dressing: In a medium bowl, whisk together the buttermilk, sour cream, and mayonnaise until smooth. Add the parsley, basil, chives, and garlic and stir to combine. Season with a pinch of salt and twist of pepper. Refrigerate until needed.

3. Grill the radicchio: In a food processor, pulse the bread until it has the consistency of coarse crumbs (larger than panko but smaller than a crouton). Pour into a medium bowl, add the olive oil, season with a pinch of salt and twist of pepper, and toss to combine. Transfer to a large cast-iron skillet, place on the hot side of the grill, and shake into an even layer. Cook, while stirring, until golden brown, about 5 minutes.

4. Drizzle the radicchio on all sides with olive oil and season with a pinch of salt and twist of pepper. Place on the hot side of the grill and cook until lightly charred but still crisp, about 1 minute per side.

5. Place the radicchio cut-side up on a platter, top with buttermilk dressing, bread crumbs, and parmesan, and serve.

Potato-Zucchini Pancakes
with Lemon Yogurt Sauce
Makes about 8 pancakes (serves 4 to 6)

Lemon Yogurt Sauce

1 cup whole-milk Greek yogurt

Grated zest and juice of ½ lemon

2 tablespoons thinly sliced fresh chives

1 tablespoon extra-virgin olive oil

Kosher salt and freshly ground black pepper

Potato-Zucchini Pancakes

2 large russet potatoes, scrubbed and grated on the large holes of a box grater

2 medium zucchini, grated on the large holes of a box grater

4 scallions, white and light-green parts only, thinly sliced (about ½ cup)

2 large eggs, lightly beaten

⅓ cup all-purpose flour

1 tablespoon finely chopped fresh dill

Kosher salt and freshly ground black pepper

Extra-virgin olive oil, for frying

One of my dad's "specialties" in the kitchen was crisp, golden-brown potato pancakes. I learned everything I needed to know about cooking potato pancakes from him, but that doesn't mean I've stopped experimenting, specifically with ways to jazz up the standard potato mixture. I often swap in any number of shredded veggies in place of all or some of the spuds, like sweet potatoes, carrots, and beets. Not only does it kick up the dish's nutritional value, it also brings a welcome twist to the flavor and texture. In the summer, when I'm looking for ways to use up some zucchini and squash from the garden, I make these. The key to keeping it crispy is to wring out as much moisture as you can from the squash prior to cooking. As a kid, we were happy with plain-old Greek yogurt or sour cream for dipping, but why not zip it up with some lemon and chives?

1. Prepare and preheat a charcoal grill for direct cooking.

2. Make the lemon yogurt sauce: In a medium bowl, whisk together the yogurt, lemon zest, lemon juice, chives, and olive oil. Season with a pinch of salt and twist of pepper. Cover and refrigerate until needed.

3. Make the potato-zucchini pancakes: Wrap the grated potatoes and zucchini in a kitchen towel and wring the vegetables out to remove as much of the liquid as you can. In a large bowl, combine the grated potato, zucchini, scallions, eggs, flour, and dill and toss to combine. Season with a pinch of salt and twist of pepper.

4. Line a large plate or platter with paper towels. Set a large cast-iron skillet on the grill. Add 1 tablespoon olive oil and heat to shimmering, then add enough of the potato and zucchini mixture to make 3 medium pancakes (about one-third of the mixture). Cook, without disturbing, until golden brown on both sides, about 2 minutes per side. Transfer to the paper towels to drain and season with salt. Repeat the process with the remaining potato mixture, adding more oil for each batch.

5. Top the pancakes with the lemon yogurt sauce and serve.

Stuffed Squash Blossoms

Serves 4

1 cup whole-milk ricotta cheese

2 tablespoons finely chopped fresh flat-leaf parsley

Grated zest of ½ lemon

Kosher salt and freshly ground black pepper

12 squash or zucchini blossoms

Neutral oil, for deep-frying

½ cup all-purpose flour

2 large eggs

One of the upsides to today's global supply chain is that most foods are available year-round. One of the downsides to that on-demand shopping world is that food feels a little less special if you don't have to wait until a certain time of year to enjoy it. Fresh squash blossoms (or squash flowers) are one of those foodstuffs that remain truly seasonal because they're best used on the day they're picked. For my money, there is no better way to prepare them than by gently filling the blossoms with seasoned ricotta, lightly breading them, and flash-frying them. If angels ate fried foods, it would be these babies.

1. Prepare and preheat a charcoal grill for direct cooking.

2. In a medium bowl, stir together the ricotta, parsley, and lemon zest. Season with a pinch of salt and twist of pepper. Stuff each zucchini blossom with 1 tablespoon of this cheese mixture, bringing the petals of the blossom up and around the cheese to seal.

3. Set a large Dutch oven on the grill. Add 3 inches of oil and heat to 350°F. Set a wire rack over a sheet pan lined with paper towels.

4. Set up a dredging station in two shallow bowls: In one bowl, whisk together the flour, a pinch of salt, and twist of pepper. Put the eggs in a second bowl and beat them lightly. Working with one blossom at a time, dredge the blossom in the flour, making sure to coat all sides well. Shake off the excess. Dip the blossom into the beaten eggs, allowing the excess to drip off. Return the blossom to the flour, turning to fully coat all sides.

5. Working in batches, if necessary, so as not to crowd the pan, fry the blossoms until golden brown and crisp, using a slotted spoon or frying spider to turn them often, about 3 minutes. Use a slotted spoon to transfer the blossoms to the rack to drain and season with salt. Serve immediately.

Creamed Leeks
with Thyme
Serves 4

3 tablespoons unsalted
butter plus 2 tablespoons
melted butter
2 large leeks, white parts
only, thinly sliced
2 tablespoons finely
chopped fresh thyme
2 teaspoons Diamond
Crystal kosher salt
2 tablespoons all-purpose
flour
1½ cups heavy cream
½ teaspoon freshly grated
nutmeg
1 cup crushed Ritz crackers
¼ cup grated pecorino
cheese

The next time you're tasked with bringing a hot snack or
appetizer to a party, leave the artichoke dip at home and bring
this instead. This creamy, comforting dish is always the first to go
when we serve it. Melty, buttery leeks are suspended in an herby
cream sauce and topped with a crunchy cracker topping. Serve it
with baguette slices—or even Ritz crackers to keep it real—and
be prepared for all the recipe requests. This would also work as
an indulgent side dish for a roast or grilled steak.

1. Prepare and preheat a charcoal grill for indirect cooking, with
   one hot side and one hold (unheated) side.

2. Set a large skillet on the hot side of the grill. Add 3 tablespoons
   of the butter, followed by the leeks, thyme, and salt. Cook, stirring
   occasionally, until the vegetables soften, about 3 minutes. Add
   the flour and cook, stirring frequently, for 2 minutes. Stirring
   constantly, slowly add the cream and nutmeg. Bring the sauce to a
   simmer and cook until slightly thickened, about 5 minutes. Remove
   from the grill.

3. In a medium bowl, combine the crackers, pecorino, and melted
   butter and stir to combine. Sprinkle this mixture on top of the
   leeks, place on the hold side of the grill, cover the grill, and cook
   until golden brown, about 30 minutes.

Creamed Corn
with Lime

Serves 4 to 6

Corn Stock

5 ears corn, shucked, kernels sliced off the cobs, cobs reserved

½ small yellow onion, quartered

1 tablespoon coriander seeds

1 teaspoon Diamond Crystal kosher salt

1 bay leaf

2 garlic cloves, smashed and peeled

Creamed Corn

1 tablespoon extra-virgin olive oil

¼ pound thick-sliced bacon, cut into ½-inch-wide pieces

2 small yellow onions, finely chopped (about 1 cup)

2 garlic cloves, minced

Kosher salt and freshly ground black pepper

½ cup sour cream or whole-milk Greek yogurt

1 tablespoon unsalted butter

½ cup finely chopped fresh cilantro

Grated zest of 1 lime

In our family, pretty much everything was made from scratch—except the creamed corn. Not only did it come from the store in a can, but we loved it that way! Later on, when I became a professional cook, I made attempts to improve upon that "Symon canned classic." After many swings at the plate, I landed on this recipe, which is guaranteed to be the best version that you've ever tasted. The not-so-secret ingredient is the corn stock, which brings a ton of deep corn flavor to the party. The other key is the bright pop of lime zest. After a million tries, I've finally cracked the can!

1. Prepare and preheat a charcoal grill for indirect cooking, with one hot side and one hold (unheated) side.

2. Make the corn stock: In a large pot, combine the corn cobs, onion, coriander, salt, bay leaf, garlic, and 8 cups cold water. Bring to a gentle boil on the hot side of the grill. Move to the hold side to maintain a gentle simmer and cook, uncovered, until the liquid has reduced to 2 cups, about 30 minutes. Strain the stock and keep warm.

3. Make the creamed corn: Line a plate with paper towels. Set a large saucepan on the hot side of the grill, add the olive oil, and heat to shimmering. Add the bacon and cook, stirring occasionally, until crisp, about 5 minutes. Using a slotted spoon, transfer to the paper towels to drain.

4. Add the onions and garlic to the saucepan and cook, stirring occasionally, until the vegetables begin to soften, about 5 minutes. Add the corn kernels, season with a pinch of salt and twist of pepper, and cook, stirring occasionally, for 5 minutes. Add the corn stock, bring to a simmer, and continue cooking until the liquid reduces and begins to thicken, about 5 minutes. Stir in the sour cream and cook for 3 minutes. Add the butter and stir until completely melted.

5. Remove the saucepan from the heat and stir in the cilantro and lime zest. Taste and adjust for seasoning, adding salt and pepper as needed. Garnish with the cooked bacon and serve.

Potato and Parmesan Churros

Makes 8

8 tablespoons (1 stick) unsalted butter
½ cup all-purpose flour
½ cup potato flour
1 teaspoon Diamond Crystal kosher salt
1 teaspoon finely chopped fresh rosemary
⅓ teaspoon baking powder
3 large eggs
½ cup freshly grated parmesan cheese
Neutral oil, for frying

If you've travelled to Mexico or Spain, you likely have enjoyed crispy fried churros, typically dusted with sugar and served alongside hot chocolate or extra-thick chocolate pudding, depending on where in the world you're enjoying them. Think of these as the savory sibling to the churro, with fresh rosemary and parmesan cheese replacing the sugar and chocolate. Churros are amazing on their own as a snack but I like to pair this version with sandwiches like the Ultimate Italian Hoagies (page 106). Step aside French fries, there's a new sheriff in town!

1. Prepare and preheat a charcoal grill for direct cooking.

2. Set a large saucepan on the grill and add 1¼ cups water and the butter. When the butter has melted, add the all-purpose flour, potato flour, salt, rosemary, and baking powder and cook, stirring constantly with a wooden spoon, until the mixture comes together, about 5 minutes.

3. Remove from the heat. Whisk in the eggs one at a time until a smooth, thick batter is formed. Whisk in 2 tablespoons of the parmesan. Transfer the batter to a pastry bag fitted with a star tip and refrigerate for at least 1 hour and up to 3 hours.

4. Prepare and preheat a charcoal grill for direct cooking.

5. Set a deep heavy-bottomed pot on the grill. Pour 4 inches of oil into the pot and heat to 325°F. Line a plate with paper towels.

6. Working in batches so as not to crowd the pan, pipe 4- to 6-inch lengths of batter into the oil, using clean shears to cut them off. Fry until golden brown and crisp, using a slotted spoon or spider strainer to turn them once, about 5 minutes total. Use a slotted spoon to transfer the churros to the paper towels to drain. Immediately sprinkle on some of the remaining 6 tablespoons parmesan cheese.

Grill-Roasted Garlic Bread

Serves 10

10 garlic cloves, peeled but whole

½ cup extra-virgin olive oil

4 tablespoons (½ stick) unsalted butter

½ teaspoon kosher salt

½ teaspoon garlic powder

1 large loaf soft Italian bread, halved horizontally

1 cup freshly grated parmesan cheese

My first real job out of culinary school was in the kitchen of Players on the west side of Cleveland. The restaurant set itself apart from other Italian bistros of the day by offering house-made breads, pastas, and pizzas. I know that garlic bread at an Italian restaurant is hardly remarkable, but we approached the dish with the same level of passion and execution that we did the nightly specials. By slowly cooking garlic cloves in olive oil, you mellow its bite, enhance its sweetness, and soften it for easy spreading. When it's good and soft, mash it with butter, spread it on the bread, and bake it over indirect heat until it melts deep into the bread. Obviously, you could use a classic Italian loaf, but this would work great with most breads.

1. Prepare and preheat a charcoal grill for indirect cooking, with one hot side and one hold (unheated) side.

2. In a small saucepan, combine the garlic and olive oil. Place on the hold side of the grill, cover the grill, and cook until the garlic is soft, about 15 minutes.

3. Remove from the heat, add the butter, and mash with the back of a fork into a thick paste. Stir in the salt and garlic powder.

4. Measure out 2 tablespoons of the garlic butter and set aside. Spread the remaining garlic butter evenly over both halves of the bread. Sprinkle the parmesan evenly over both halves of the bread. Place the bread butter-side up on a sheet pan, put it on the hold side, cover the grill, and cook until the bread is crisp and the cheese is browned, about 10 minutes.

5. Put the two bread halves together and slice the loaf into 10 equal pieces. Arrange them on a platter, brush with the reserved garlic butter, and serve.

My Favorite Asparagus

Serves 4

Grated zest and juice of
1 lemon

1 tablespoon whole-grain
mustard

1 teaspoon prepared
horseradish

¼ cup extra-virgin olive oil,
plus more for drizzling

Kosher salt and freshly
ground black pepper

2 large bunches of thick
green asparagus

2 heads red Belgian endive,
halved and cored

1 large yellow onion, sliced
into ½-inch-thick rings

I think the reason why a lot of people turn their nose up at asparagus is the same reason people do for a lot of vegetables: They're often hopelessly overcooked. Asparagus is one of the first harbingers of spring, an event that I look forward to every year. I make a point of visiting the local farmers' markets to snatch up those first tender shoots. Most of the time, I just drizzle them with olive oil, season, and lightly grill, which brings out the sweetness while retaining a pleasantly crisp but tender bite. When I'm looking for something a little more impressive, I make them this way. If you've lost countless asparagus to the grill gods through those pesky grates, cooking them on a sheet pan will save you, while still introducing a light smokiness.

1. Prepare and preheat a charcoal grill for direct cooking.

2. In a medium bowl, whisk together the lemon zest, lemon juice, mustard, horseradish, and olive oil. Season with a pinch of salt and twist of pepper. Set the dressing aside.

3. Arrange the asparagus, endive, and onion rings on a sheet pan. Drizzle with olive oil, season with a pinch of salt and twist of pepper, and toss to coat.

4. Place on the grill and cook, uncovered, stirring halfway, until lightly browned but still crisp-tender, about 4 minutes.

5. Transfer to a platter, top with the dressing, and serve.

Duck Fat-Fried Fondant Potatoes

Serves 4

2 pounds medium Yukon
   Gold potatoes, peeled
Kosher salt and freshly
   ground black pepper
2 tablespoons duck fat,
   bacon fat, or olive oil
4 tablespoons (½ stick)
   unsalted butter
5 sprigs of thyme
2 garlic cloves, skin on and
   smashed
1 cup chicken stock
Smoked flaky sea salt, for
   serving

Fondant potatoes are having a moment, with viral videos popping up all over the socials. Made by searing and then gently simmering the spuds, they offer the perfect yin-yang of crispy, golden brown exterior and pillowy potato core. I do it on the grill, and the results are dreamy. Maybe it's just me, but I find the fiery heat from below produces the ideal crust. I finish them with a sprinkle of flaky smoked sea salt for an added kick. If you don't have access to duck fat, you can substitute bacon fat or any neutral oil, but you do need something to mix with the butter to raise the smoke point. If you really want to punch up the presentation, use a 1½-inch ring cutter to make perfect scallop-shape potatoes. Yes, these take a little finesse to get perfect, but I think they're worth it.

1. Prepare and preheat a charcoal grill for direct cooking. Adjust the grill vents to maintain a temperature of 350° to 400°F (see Controlling the Grill Temperature, page 17).

2. Trim off the ends of the potatoes and cut them in half crosswise so that they resemble large scallops. (Alternatively, you can use a 1½-inch biscuit cutter.) Season all sides liberally with pinches of kosher salt and twists of black pepper.

3. Set a large cast-iron skillet on the grill. Add the duck fat and 2 tablespoons of the butter and heat to shimmering. Add the potatoes in a single layer and cook, without disturbing, until golden brown on both sides, about 3 minutes per side. Add the thyme and garlic. Carefully tilt the skillet and use a spoon to baste the potatoes with the fat. Add the chicken stock and bring to a simmer. Add the remaining 2 tablespoons butter, move the skillet to the hold side of the grill, cover the grill, and cook until the potatoes are easily pierced by a fork, basting halfway through, about 35 minutes.

4. Remove the skillet from the grill and baste the potatoes one final time. Transfer the potatoes to a platter (discarding the thyme sprigs and garlic), drizzle on some of the pan sauce, garnish with smoked sea salt, and serve.

Grilled Greens
with Lime Vinaigrette
Serves 4 to 6

Lime Vinaigrette
Juice of 2 limes
2 garlic cloves, grated
4 white anchovies, finely
  chopped
1 tablespoon Dijon mustard
1 teaspoon red pepper
  flakes
½ cup extra-virgin olive oil
Kosher salt and freshly
  ground black pepper

Croutons
8 tablespoons (1 stick)
  unsalted butter
1 garlic clove, peeled but
  whole
1 small baguette, torn into
  1-inch pieces
Kosher salt and freshly
  ground black pepper

Grilled Greens
1 head red Belgian endive,
  halved lengthwise
1 head escarole, outer
  leaves removed, halved
  lengthwise
2 pounds lacinato kale,
  stemmed
1 cup thinly sliced fresh
  chives, for serving
Freshly grated parmesan
  cheese, for serving

Now this is a salad "that eats like a meal." It's built atop a trio of grilled greens, each with its own texture and flavor. After grilling, the lettuces are tossed in a classic vinaigrette punched up with lime and anchovy. The icing on the cake, so to speak, are the crunchy, buttery, garlicky croutons. You can experiment with any type of head lettuce that you'd like here, such as romaine, radicchio, and Little Gem.

1. Prepare and preheat a charcoal grill for indirect cooking, with one hot side and one hold (unheated) side. Adjust the grill vents to maintain a temperature of 350°F (see Controlling the Grill Temperature, page 17).

2. Make the lime vinaigrette: In a medium bowl, whisk together the lime juice, garlic, anchovies, mustard, pepper flakes, and olive oil. Season with a few pinches of salt and twists of pepper. Set aside until needed.

3. Make the croutons: Set a small saucepan on the hot side of the grill and add the butter and garlic. Place the baguette pieces in a medium bowl. When the butter has melted, pour it and the garlic over the baguette and toss to fully coat. Season with a few pinches of salt and twists of pepper.

4. Place the bread in a large cast-iron skillet, set it on the hot side of the grill, cover the grill, and cook without stirring until golden brown and crisp, about 7 minutes. Set aside.

5. Grill the greens: Brush the cut sides of the endive and escarole with the vinaigrette, place cut-side down on the hot side of the grill, and cook until nicely charred, about 2 minutes. Remove from the grill to cool slightly before roughly chopping and transferring to a large salad bowl.

6. In a large bowl, toss the kale leaves with 2 tablespoons of the vinaigrette to coat. Place the leaves on the hot side of the grill and cook until lightly charred, about 1 minute per side. Transfer to the bowl with the endive and escarole.

7. Top the salad with the croutons, chives, and parmesan and toss to combine. Serve with any remaining vinaigrette.

Grilled Squash
with Hot Pepper Olive Relish
Serves 4

4 medium yellow squash and/or zucchini, cut into ⅓-inch-thick slices

4 tablespoons extra-virgin olive oil

Kosher salt and freshly ground black pepper

2 jalapeños, thinly sliced into rings

2 anchovy fillets

1 garlic clove, thinly sliced

12 green olives (I like Cerignola), pitted and halved

¼ cup roughly chopped fresh flat-leaf parsley

¼ cup roughly chopped fresh mint

1 teaspoon red pepper flakes

Grated zest and juice of 1 lemon

This Mediterranean grilled squash dish offers a riot of colors, flavors, and textures. It's as impressive to look at as it is to eat—and it couldn't be more wholesome. Start with in-season squash that hasn't gotten too big and grill it fast over a hot fire. Buttery and meaty green olives like Castelvetrano or Cerignola are gently heated to bring out their aroma, paired with lemon zest and a bounty of fresh herbs, and then spooned over the grilled squash. I like to serve this with whole grilled fish, but it really goes with anything. It's just as delicious at room temperature as it is when hot.

1. Prepare and preheat a charcoal grill for direct cooking. Set a large perforated pan on the grill.

2. In a medium bowl, toss the squash with 2 tablespoons of the olive oil to coat. Season with a pinch of salt and twist of pepper.

3. Place the squash on the perforated pan and cook until lightly charred, about 2 minutes per side. Transfer to a platter.

4. Set a small saucepan on the grill, add the remaining 2 tablespoons olive oil, and heat to shimmering. Add the jalapeños, anchovies, and garlic and cook, stirring occasionally, until the anchovies dissolve, about 1 minute. Add the olives and cook for 1 minute. Remove from the grill and stir in the parsley, mint, pepper flakes, lemon zest, and lemon juice.

5. Spoon the sauce over the grilled squash and serve.

Twice-Fried Plantains
with Lime Crema
Serves 4

2 green plantains
Neutral oil, for deep-frying
Kosher salt
½ cup Mexican crema or
    sour cream
Grated zest and juice
    of 2 limes
1 cup fresh cilantro leaves
2 scallions, white and light-
    green parts only, thinly
    sliced (about ¼ cup)

These golden-brown plantain chips—commonly referred to as tostones—are a great substitute for the tortilla chips that typically accompany guacamole. But they can just as easily stand in for ho-hum starches like rice, potatoes, and polenta when you're looking for a change of pace. Green plantains have become more widely available around the country, but if your grocery store doesn't carry them, look for a Latin market. Personally, I love frying these in bacon or duck fat and serving them with scrambled eggs at breakfast or brunch. Yum!

1. Prepare and preheat a charcoal grill for direct cooking.

2. Peel the plantains by trimming an inch off both ends, slicing the peel lengthwise (try not going too deep into the flesh), and removing the peel. Cut into 2-inch-thick slices and set aside.

3. Set a deep heavy-bottomed pot on the grill. Add 4 inches of oil and heat to 360°F. Set a wire rack over a sheet pan lined with paper towels.

4. Working in batches so as not to crowd the pan, fry the plantains until golden brown, using a slotted spoon or spider strainer to turn them halfway, about 6 minutes total. Use a slotted spoon to transfer the plantains to the rack and season with a few pinches of salt. Set aside until cool enough to handle.

5. Working with 1 slice of plantain at a time, place between 2 sheets of parchment paper and use the bottom of a small skillet to press the slice to a thickness of ¼ inch. Working in batches again, return the pressed plantains to the hot oil and fry until very crispy on both sides, about 2 minutes total. Return them to the wire rack as they finish.

6. In a small bowl, whisk together the crema and lime juice.

7. Transfer the fried plantains to a platter, drizzle with lime crema, garnish with cilantro, scallions, and lime zest, and serve.

Grill-Roasted Tomatoes
with Herby Bread Crumbs

Serves 4

1 cup panko bread crumbs

¾ cup extra-virgin olive oil, plus more for greasing

¼ cup freshly grated parmesan cheese

1 tablespoon finely chopped fresh oregano

1 tablespoon finely chopped fresh rosemary

1 tablespoon finely chopped fresh flat-leaf parsley

1 tablespoon finely chopped fresh thyme

Kosher salt and freshly ground black pepper

2 large beefsteak tomatoes, cored and cut into 1-inch-thick slices

Small loaf of rustic bread, cut into 4 (¾-inch-thick) slices

When you are inundated with juicy-ripe tomatoes from your garden or local farmers' market, give this recipe a whirl. I know some people don't like cooked tomatoes, but these take on such great flavor and texture from the herby topping. Serve them with any protein coming off the grill or just pair them with some grilled bread, nice cheese, and a bottle of crisp white wine.

1. Prepare and preheat a charcoal grill for indirect cooking, with one hot side and one hold (unheated) side.

2. In a medium bowl, combine the panko, ¼ cup of the olive oil, the parmesan, oregano, rosemary, parsley, and thyme. Season with a pinch of salt and twist of pepper and toss to combine.

3. Set a large cast-iron skillet on the hold side of the grill and grease with olive oil. Add the tomatoes and season liberally with salt. Spread the herby panko mixture evenly on top. Cover the grill and cook until the tomatoes have softened and the topping is golden brown, about 8 minutes.

4. Meanwhile, brush both sides of each slice of bread with 2 tablespoons olive oil, season with salt and pepper, and place on the grill. Cook until slightly charred and toasted on both sides, about 30 seconds per side. Serve the tomatoes with the grilled bread.

Blue Corn Bread
with Honey Butter

Serves 4

Honey Butter

8 tablespoons (1 stick) unsalted butter, at room temperature

¼ cup raw honey

½ teaspoon pure vanilla extract

¼ teaspoon ground cinnamon or smoked cinnamon

Corn Bread

1 cup whole milk

⅓ cup unsalted butter, melted

1 large egg, separated

1 cup stone-ground blue cornmeal (I like Anson Mills)

1 cup all-purpose flour

⅓ cup sugar

3½ tablespoons baking powder

1 tablespoon Diamond Crystal kosher salt

1 teaspoon cornstarch

Cooking spray

This recipe was inspired by the corn bread that Liz and I enjoyed one evening at Hatchet Hall in Culver City, California. It was so good that the hair on my arm literally stood up and I may have shed a tear! It was my all time favorite restaurant corn bread and this is my attempt at re-creating that magical dish. One of the things that makes their preparation unique is the final inversion after baking, so that the crusty bottom of the corn bread is presented as the top. Then it's dolloped with a sexy honey butter that melts into the warm bread. There goes the hair on my arm again!!

1. Make the honey butter: In a medium bowl, whisk together the butter, honey, vanilla, and cinnamon. Cover and refrigerate until needed.

2. Prepare and preheat a charcoal grill for indirect cooking, with one hot side and one hold (unheated) side. Adjust the grill vents to maintain a temperature of 425°F (see Controlling the Grill Temperature, page 17).

3. Make the corn bread: In a large bowl, whisk together the milk, melted butter, and egg yolk. In a separate large bowl, whisk together the cornmeal, flour, sugar, baking powder, and salt. Add the wet ingredients to the dry ingredients and whisk until just combined. In a separate medium bowl, whisk the egg white and cornstarch until the whites form stiff, shiny peaks, about 5 minutes. Use a silicone spatula to gently fold the egg whites into the batter.

4. Set a large cast-iron skillet on the hot side of the grill to preheat. Remove from the grill and generously grease the bottom and sides with cooking spray. Pour the batter into the skillet and place on the hold side of the grill. Cover the grill and cook until golden brown and a toothpick inserted into the center comes out clean, about 25 minutes.

5. Remove from the grill and carefully invert the corn bread onto a platter. Spread some honey butter on the top (previously the bottom) of the corn bread and serve immediately with more on the side.

Rye Spaetzle
with Brown Butter

Serves 4

1 cup whole milk
4 large eggs
1 tablespoon sour cream
1 tablespoon Dijon mustard
1 tablespoon thinly sliced
    fresh chives
1 teaspoon ground caraway
Kosher salt and freshly
    ground black pepper
2 cups all-purpose flour
1 cup rye flour
4 tablespoons (½ stick)
    unsalted butter

In this little riff on my grandfather's spaetzle, we swap some of the all-purpose flour for rye flour, which imparts a hint of that aromatic grain. The addition of ground caraway adds another layer of complexity. The combination of earthy rye and peppery caraway makes this side dish a natural for grilled foods. Serve these guys anywhere you would use regular spaetzle, but I especially like to serve them with grilled pork chops or sausages.

1. Prepare and preheat a charcoal grill for direct cooking.

2. In a large bowl, whisk together the milk, eggs, sour cream, mustard, chives, caraway, and 1 teaspoon Diamond Crystal kosher salt. Season with a few twists of black pepper. Add the all-purpose and rye flours and stir with a wooden spoon to form a sticky batter. Cover and refrigerate for 30 minutes.

3. Add 2 tablespoons of salt to a medium pot of water and bring to a boil on the grill.

4. Use a spaetzle maker to push the batter into the boiling water (you may have to do this in batches so as not to overcrowd the pot). Once the spaetzle floats, after about 1 minute, continue cooking for 1 minute more.

5. In a large skillet, melt the butter over medium heat and cook, stirring, until the butter begins to brown and smell nutty, about 5 minutes. Using a slotted spoon, transfer the spaetzle to the skillet, along with ½ cup of the cooking water. Stir to combine and serve immediately.

Butternut Squash Gratin

Serves 4

3 tablespoons unsalted butter

2 leeks, white parts only, halved lengthwise and thinly sliced

Kosher salt and freshly ground black pepper

3 garlic cloves, minced

2 tablespoons fresh thyme leaves

1 teaspoon chipotle powder

1 teaspoon sweet paprika

1 teaspoon freshly grated nutmeg

1 cup heavy cream

1 (2-pound) butternut squash, peeled, seeded, and cut crosswise into ¼-inch-thick slices

1 cup shredded Gruyère cheese

2 cups panko bread crumbs

1 cup freshly grated parmesan cheese

3 tablespoons thinly sliced fresh chives, for garnish

The possibilities truly are endless when it comes to vegetable gratin dishes. The time-tested formula of vegetable, cream sauce, and crispy topping can be tweaked and adjusted to your heart's content—and I have countless personal favorites. This recipe is ideal for fall, when winter squashes like butternut, acorn, pumpkin, and delicata are abundant. Any of those, by the way, can be swapped into this recipe. If the slightly smoky-spicy flavor of chipotle is not your favorite, leave it out.

1. Prepare and preheat a charcoal grill for indirect cooking, with one hot side and one hold (unheated) side. Adjust the grill vents to maintain a temperature of 350° to 400°F (see Controlling the Grill Temperature, page 17).

2. Set a large saucepan on the hot side of the grill and melt the butter. Add the leeks and a pinch of salt and cook, stirring occasionally, until the leeks begin to soften and brown, about 3 minutes. Add the garlic, thyme, chipotle, paprika, and nutmeg and cook, stirring occasionally, for 1 minute until fragrant. Add the cream and bring to a simmer. Taste and adjust for seasoning, adding salt and pepper as needed.

3. Arrange one-third of the squash in an even layer in a 9 × 13-inch metal baking pan or grill-safe ceramic baking dish. Top with one-third of the leek and cream mixture. Top with one-third of the Gruyère. Repeat the process with the remaining squash, leek and cream mixture, and Gruyère. In a medium bowl, stir to combine the panko and parmesan. Sprinkle this mixture on top of the casserole.

4. Cover the pan with foil, place on the hold side of the grill, cover the grill, and cook for 30 minutes.

5. Remove the foil and cook until the top is golden brown, about 5 minutes. Let set for 10 minutes before garnishing with chives and serving.

Celery Root Pancakes

Serves 4

2 large eggs

1 tablespoon Dijon mustard

2 large celery roots, peeled and grated on the large holes of a box grater

6 scallions, white and light-green parts only, thinly sliced (about ¾ cup)

2 tablespoons finely chopped fresh dill

Kosher salt and freshly ground black pepper

1 cup rice flour

4 tablespoons extra-virgin olive oil

Flaky sea salt, for serving

Here's another twist on the classic potato pancakes that we enjoyed while growing up in the Symon household. I'm always looking for ways to utilize underappreciated vegetables like celery root, which has a beautiful but mild celery-like flavor. You can go with 100-percent celery root as I do here, or you can mix it with potato, sweet potato, or even carrot. I think these would go great with Quick Smoked Duck Breast (page 178).

1. Prepare and preheat a charcoal grill for direct cooking.

2. In a large bowl, whisk together the eggs and mustard. Add the celery root, scallions, and dill to the egg/mustard mixture and stir to combine. Season with a pinch of kosher salt and twist of pepper and toss to combine. Add the rice flour and toss to combine.

3. Set a large skillet on the grill to preheat. Line a large plate or platter with paper towels. Add 2 tablespoons of the olive oil to the skillet and heat to shimmering. Add enough of the celery root mixture to make 4 medium pancakes (about half of the mixture). Cook, without disturbing, until golden brown, about 2 minutes per side. Transfer to the paper towels to drain. Repeat the process with the remaining 2 tablespoons olive oil and the remaining celery root mixture.

4. Top with sea salt and serve immediately.

Ultimate Cheesy Hash Browns

Makes 8 squares

2 large russet potatoes,
   scrubbed
3 tablespoons rice flour
2 tablespoons cornstarch
1 tablespoon whole milk
Kosher salt and freshly
   ground black pepper
8 slices low-moisture
   mozzarella cheese
Neutral oil, for frying

Apart from my dad's regular trips to McDonald's for a hot cup of joe, we definitely were not a fast-food family. For the most part, nothing has changed for me in my adult years. But I'm not going to lie and say that I never eat fast food. If I do, it most likely comes in the form of a quick breakfast while I'm on the road filming and have zero free time. And when I do, who can resist the siren song of a hot, crisp, golden-brown hash brown patty?! These cheese-stuffed hash browns take the game to a whole new level by sandwiching melty mozzarella between two ridiculously crispy-crunchy cakes. It's a bit of work, but you may never hit the drive-through again! You can make these ahead and freeze them before frying, but add a couple minutes to the cook time.

1. Prepare and preheat a charcoal grill for indirect cooking, with one hot side and one hold (unheated) side. Adjust the grill vents to maintain a temperature of 350°F (see Controlling the Grill Temperature, page 17).

2. Place the potatoes on the hot side of the grill, cover the grill, and cook until just tender enough to pierce with a fork, about 40 minutes. Set aside to cool for 30 minutes.

3. Peel the potatoes and grate them on the large holes of a box grater into a large bowl. Add the rice flour, cornstarch, and milk. Season with a pinch of salt and twist of pepper and toss to combine. Place the potatoes on a large piece of parchment paper and press into a rough square. Top with a second piece of parchment paper and, using a rolling pin, roll the potatoes out to a thickness of ⅛ inch. Using a sharp knife, cut the potato cake into 16 equal squares.

4. Fold the mozzarella slices in quarters so that, when placed in the center of a potato cake, they leave a border of potato. Working with 1 potato cake at a time, place a slice of cheese in the center of the potato cake, top with a second potato cake, and press to join and seal the pieces. Cover and refrigerate for at least 1 hour and up to overnight.

5. Set a deep heavy-bottomed pot on the grill. Add 4 inches of oil and heat to 360°F. Set a wire rack over a sheet pan lined with paper towels.

6. Working in batches so as not to crowd the pan, fry the potato cakes until golden brown, using a slotted spoon or spider strainer to turn them halfway, about 2 minutes per side. Use a slotted spoon to transfer the hash browns to the rack, season with a few pinches of salt and twists of black pepper, and serve.

3

Quick and Easy

When pressed for time, we often don't make the best decisions about what to eat. That's when we reach for a pizza from the freezer, or worse, hit the drive-through on the way home from work. I'm here to argue that "quick and easy" doesn't have to mean bland and boring. This chapter is loaded with recipes that require limited ingredients and brief amounts of time to get delicious food on the table. Even chefs—*especially chefs!*—don't want to spend hours in the kitchen after a long day or work, parenting, or, in my case, grandparenting.

Don't let the "quick and easy" part fool you: There are plenty of recipes here with flavors that will knock your socks off. Any meal that includes Oysters Casino (page 110) or Smoked Trout with Arugula, Dill, and Lemon (page 116) will feel like a celebration, whether it's a Saturday or a Monday. For big appetites, bust out the Ultimate Italian Hoagies (page 106) or Gyro-Style Lamb Burgers with Tzatziki and Grilled Onion (page 124) and prepare to be thoroughly satisfied. If you grew up in Cleveland as I did, you likely have fond memories of a dish called City Chicken Skewers (page 133), which is in fact pork and totally amazing. In fact, most food tastes better when it's threaded on a skewer and cooked over charcoal, like the Grilled Chicken Souvlaki (page 130) in this chapter.

Grilled Flank Steak
with Pepper Relish
Serves 4

4 (8-ounce) flank steaks
¼ cup packed light brown
   sugar
¼ cup yellow mustard
¼ cup soy sauce
Kosher salt and freshly
   ground black pepper

Pepper Relish
6 tablespoons extra-virgin
   olive oil
1 medium red bell pepper,
   roughly chopped (about
   1 cup)
1 medium yellow bell
   pepper, roughly chopped
   (about 1 cup)
1 small red onion, halved
   and thinly sliced (about
   ½ cup)
1 jalapeño, seeded and
   minced
2 garlic cloves, minced
1 tablespoon finely chopped
   fresh thyme
Kosher salt and freshly
   ground black pepper
¼ cup sherry vinegar
Grated zest and juice
   of 1 lime
¼ cup raw honey
¼ cup finely chopped fresh
   cilantro

I grill more flank and skirt steak than pretty much any other cut of beef. While you give up a little bit of tenderness you gain it back in spades with respect to flavor. And given that it's much less expensive than upmarket cuts, you can enjoy it more often. Flank steak always benefits from a nice marinade (I add a hint of soy for that all-important umami!) and don't forget to let it rest after grilling before slicing it thinly and against the grain for the most tender bite. I recommend not cooking this cut past medium, as it tends to get too chewy.

1. Pierce the flank steaks with a fork or paring knife a few times on both sides. Place the steaks in a 1-gallon zip-top bag. In a small bowl, whisk together the brown sugar, mustard, and soy sauce. Season with a pinch of salt and twist of black pepper. Pour the marinade over the steaks and let marinate at room temperature for 1 hour.

2. Prepare and preheat a charcoal grill for direct cooking.

3. Remove the steaks from the bag, allowing most of the marinade to drip off (discard the marinade). Put the steaks on the grill and cook, without moving, until nicely charred, about 4 minutes. Flip and continue cooking until nicely charred and medium-rare (130°F), about 4 minutes.

4. Transfer the steaks to a cutting board to rest, loosely tented with foil, for 10 minutes.

5. While the steaks are resting, make the pepper relish: Set a large cast-iron skillet on the grill. Add 2 tablespoons of the olive oil and heat to shimmering. Add the red and yellow bell peppers, onions, jalapeño, garlic, and thyme. Season with a pinch of salt and twist of pepper. Cook, stirring occasionally, until the vegetables are aromatic and begin to soften, about 5 minutes. Add the vinegar and lime juice and cook until the liquid is reduced by half, about 5 minutes. Remove from the heat and stir in the honey, cilantro, the remaining 4 tablespoons olive oil, and the lime zest.

6. Slice the steaks thinly against the grain, top with pepper relish, and serve.

Ultimate Italian Hoagies

Makes 4 hoagies

4 (12-inch) sesame semolina hoagie/hero/sub rolls, partially split

¾ pound thinly sliced mortadella

¾ pound thinly sliced hard salami

¾ pound thinly sliced capicola

¾ pound thinly sliced soppressata

¾ pound shredded aged provolone cheese

6 ounces freshly grated pecorino cheese

¼ cup red wine vinegar

2 tablespoons dried Sicilian oregano

1 garlic clove, grated

½ cup extra-virgin olive oil

Kosher salt and freshly ground black pepper

1 head escarole, outer leaves removed, thinly sliced crosswise to the core

1 large red onion, halved and thinly sliced (about 1 cup)

1 large tomato, thinly sliced

2 cups fresh basil leaves

My first restaurant job growing up was at Geppetto's, a pizza shop in Cleveland. The pizza was fine, but more often than not, it was the Italian hoagie that was in my hands. Piled high with sliced deli meats, capped with cheese, and baked until melty and toasty, these sandwiches were my favorites at lunchtime. I've been a sandwich lover ever since. Like the one that kickstarted my obsession, this one is piled high with Italian salumi, topped with provolone, and baked until golden brown. In place of the standard-issue vinaigrette, I add a bright and perky escarole salad.

1. Prepare and preheat a charcoal grill for indirect cooking, with one hot side and one hold (unheated) side. Adjust the grill vents to maintain a temperature of 350° to 400°F (see Controlling the Grill Temperature, page 17).

2. Open (but don't separate) the rolls. Divide the mortadella, salami, capicola, and soppressata equally among the rolls, placing the meat right in the middle of the two halves of bread. Top the meat in each roll with one-quarter of the provolone and one-quarter of the pecorino. Transfer the sandwiches to a sheet pan, place on the hold side of the grill, cover the grill, and cook until the cheese is melted, about 5 minutes.

3. In a medium bowl, whisk together the vinegar, oregano, garlic, and olive oil. Season with a pinch of salt and twist of pepper. Add the escarole and onions and toss to combine.

4. Remove the sandwiches from the grill. Divide the escarole salad equally among the sandwiches, top with tomato slices and fresh basil, close the sandwiches, and serve.

Smoky Portobello Cheesesteaks

Serves 4

6 tablespoons extra-virgin olive oil

2 tablespoons balsamic vinegar

1 tablespoon finely chopped fresh oregano

Kosher salt and freshly ground black pepper

4 large portobello mushrooms, stemmed

2 tablespoons unsalted butter

3 large yellow onions, halved and thinly sliced (about 3 cups)

12 slices provolone cheese

4 (10-inch) hoagie/hero/ sub rolls

I could polish off a foot-long Philly cheesesteak every day of the year, but that probably wouldn't be a great idea (if you know, you know). This fun riff on the classic swaps out the shaved rib eye for meaty grilled mushrooms, which provide a surprising amount of savory goodness. The sliced shrooms get packed into a warm hoagie bun with buttery grilled onions and melty provolone cheese. These two-fisted beauts will have you thinking you're in South Philly.

1. Prepare and preheat a charcoal grill for indirect cooking, with one hot side and one hold (unheated) side.

2. In a medium bowl, whisk together the olive oil, vinegar, and oregano. Season with a pinch of salt and twist of pepper. Add the portobellos and toss to coat. Set aside for 5 minutes to marinate.

3. Set a large cast-iron skillet on the hot side of the grill and add the butter. When the butter has melted, add the onions and a pinch of salt. At the same time, place the mushrooms, gill-side down, on the hold side of the grill. Cover the grill and cook for 5 minutes.

4. Flip the mushrooms and give the onions a stir. Continue cooking the mushrooms until lightly charred, about 5 minutes. Transfer the mushrooms to a cutting board and thinly slice them. Add the sliced mushrooms to the skillet with the onions.

5. Arrange the vegetables in the pan to form 4 equal piles. Top each pile with 3 slices of provolone. Place the hoagie buns on the hold side of the grill, cover the grill, and cook until the cheese melts, about 3 minutes.

6. Using a metal spatula, lift each stack off the pan and stuff into a warmed hoagie bun and serve.

Oysters Casino

Makes 12 (serves 4)

½ pound pancetta, finely chopped

1 cup panko bread crumbs

1 tablespoon extra-virgin olive oil, plus more if needed

1 medium shallot, finely chopped

2 garlic cloves, minced

2 sticks (8 ounces) unsalted butter, at room temperature

½ teaspoon red pepper flakes

½ cup freshly grated parmesan cheese

2 tablespoons finely chopped fresh flat-leaf parsley

Grated zest of 1 lemon

12 raw oysters on the half shell

There are two types of people in this world: Those who don't eat raw oysters, and my friends. I kid, I kid!! I get it, not everyone loves the taste and texture of a freshly shucked oyster. Thankfully, there are a ton of amazing ways to cook them, from crispy deep-fried oysters to famous New Orleans–style char-grilled oysters. This is one of my favorite ways to enjoy them (other than raw!). It's a play on the classic shellfish starter, Clams Casino. If you've never bought whole, unshucked oysters from the market, now is your chance. Get yourself an oyster knife, watch a couple YouTube videos, practice carefully, and have some fun!

1. Prepare and preheat a charcoal grill for indirect cooking, with one hot side and one hold (unheated) side.

2. Set a large cast-iron skillet on the hot side of the grill. Add the pancetta and cook, stirring occasionally, until the pancetta is very crisp, about 7 minutes. Use a slotted spoon to transfer the pancetta to a medium bowl, leaving the fat in the pan.

3. To the same skillet, add the panko and cook, stirring constantly, until golden brown, about 3 minutes. If the pan appears too dry, drizzle in a little olive oil. Set aside the toasted panko.

4. To the same skillet, add 1 tablespoon olive oil and heat to shimmering. Add the shallot and garlic and cook, stirring occasionally, until the vegetables soften, about 3 minutes. Transfer to the bowl with the pancetta. Add the butter and pepper flakes and stir to combine.

5. In a medium bowl, stir together the parmesan, parsley, lemon zest, and the toasted panko.

6. Divide the butter mixture evenly among the 12 oysters. Set the oysters directly on the grill grates, cover the grill, and cook until the butter has fully melted, about 3 minutes.

7. Divide the seasoned panko mixture among the oysters, cover the grill, and cook until golden brown, about 2 minutes. Serve immediately.

Pan-Fried Mozzarella Sandwiches with Tomato Salad

Serves 4

Tomato Salad

½ cup extra-virgin olive oil
¼ cup red wine vinegar
Kosher salt and freshly
    ground black pepper
2 large heirloom tomatoes,
    large diced
2 cups loosely packed fresh
    basil leaves
1 small red onion, halved
    and thinly sliced (about
    ½ cup)

Mozzarella Sandwiches

Olive oil, for frying
8 slices white sandwich
    bread, crusts removed
1 (8-ounce) ball fresh
    mozzarella, cut into
    4 slices
8 brown anchovies
    (optional)
1 cup all-purpose flour
Kosher salt and freshly
    ground black pepper
4 large eggs
¼ cup whole milk
1 cup fine dried bread
    crumbs or panko

The original fried mozzarella looks and tastes nothing like the greasy breaded "sticks" that arrive in a wax paper–lined basket at the local pub. Invented two hundred years ago in Naples, *mozzarella in carrozza* is more like a crispy "grilled" cheese sandwich that gets dipped in an egg wash and coated in bread crumbs prior to pan-frying. Overseas you can expect to find versions made with buffalo mozzarella, ham, and/or anchovies. I think the anchovies are essential in balancing the richness of the cheese, but you can omit them if you want. These comforting hot pockets of cheese are often served with marinara, but I prefer a refreshing tomato and basil salad to help cut the richness of the sandwich.

1. Prepare and preheat a charcoal grill for direct cooking.

2. Make the tomato salad: In a medium bowl, whisk together the olive oil and vinegar. Season with a pinch of salt and twist of pepper. Add the tomatoes, basil, and onion and toss to combine.

3. Assemble the mozzarella sandwiches: Set a large, deep cast-iron skillet on the grill. Add 1 inch of olive oil and heat to 350°F.

4. Top each of 4 bread slices with 1 slice mozzarella and 2 anchovies (if using). Top the sandwiches with the other slice of bread and press the edges firmly to seal.

5. Set up a dredging station in three shallow bowls: Put the flour in one bowl and season with a pinch of salt and twist of pepper. Put the eggs and milk in a second bowl and beat them lightly. Put the bread crumbs in the third bowl and season with a pinch of salt and twist of pepper.

6. Working with one sandwich at a time, dredge the sandwich in the flour, making sure to coat both sides well. Shake off the excess. Dip the sandwich into the beaten eggs, allowing the excess to drip off. Finally, lay the sandwich in the bread crumbs, turning and pressing to fully coat both sides.

7. Line a plate with paper towels. Working in batches so as not to crowd the pan, fry the sandwiches until golden brown, about 2 minutes per side. Use a slotted spoon to transfer the fried sandwiches to the paper towels to drain.

8. Cut the fried mozzarella sandwiches in half and serve with the tomato salad.

Sloppy Joe Tacos

Serves 6

3 tablespoons extra-virgin olive oil

2 pounds ground meat (turkey, lamb, pork, beef, or chicken)

1 teaspoon smoked paprika

½ teaspoon ground cumin

Kosher salt and freshly ground black pepper

1 small yellow onion, roughly chopped (about ½ cup)

2 garlic cloves, minced

1 cup chicken stock

1 cup canned crushed tomatoes

¼ cup yellow mustard

¼ cup packed light brown sugar (optional)

6 corn or flour tortillas

Optional Toppings

Diced avocado

Chopped tomatoes

Fresh cilantro leaves

Lime wedges

Sliced radishes

Shaved cabbage

Sliced jalapeños

Hot sauce

I love Sloppy Joes and I love tacos, so why not marry them together in (un)holy matrimony? This is just a fun, easy, and easy-to-enjoy recipe that could easily be bumped up to feed a crowd. You can set up a little "sloppy taco" bar, loaded with warm tortillas, a mix of fresh toppings, lime wedges, and hot sauces. Who knows, maybe we can start a Sloppy Joe Taco Tuesday trend?

1. Prepare and preheat a charcoal grill for indirect cooking, with one hot side and one hold (unheated) side.

2. Set a large cast-iron skillet on the hot side of the grill. Add the olive oil and heat to shimmering. Add the ground meat, smoked paprika, cumin, a pinch of salt, and twist of pepper. Cook, stirring with a wooden spoon to break up the meat, until lightly browned, about 5 minutes. Add the onion and garlic and cook, stirring occasionally, until the vegetables begin to soften, about 2 minutes.

3. Add the chicken stock, crushed tomatoes, mustard, and brown sugar (if using) and cook, stirring occasionally, for 5 minutes.

4. Meanwhile, wrap the tortillas in foil and place on the hold side of the grill to warm for 5 minutes.

5. Transfer the Sloppy Joe mixture to a bowl and serve with warm tortillas and toppings.

Smoked Trout
with Arugula, Dill, and Lemon
Serves 4

2 tablespoons Diamond Crystal kosher salt, plus more to taste

2 tablespoons light brown sugar

4 skin-on trout fillets (4 to 6 ounces each)

8 tablespoons extra-virgin olive oil

Small loaf of rustic bread, cut into 4 (¾-inch-thick) slices

Juice of 2 lemons

2 tablespoons capers, drained

Freshly ground black pepper

4 cups loosely packed arugula

1 medium red onion, halved and thinly sliced (about 1 cup)

1 cup roughly chopped fresh dill

There is no such thing as too much smoked fish, especially trout and whitefish. Here the indirect heat of the burning charcoal provides a mild, gentle smoke to the fish. Not only does the process enhance the flavor and texture of many varieties, but it also greatly extends the shelf life. Smoked fish is extremely versatile in the kitchen, with options ranging from smoked-fish dips and spreads to soft-scrambled eggs with smoked fish and chives. The easiest (and best) way to enjoy it is a simple salad with greens, fresh herbs, and a lemony vinaigrette.

1. In a large, flat glass dish that will hold the fish in a single layer, combine the salt, brown sugar, and 4 cups water and whisk to dissolve the salt and sugar. Add the trout skin-side up, cover, and refrigerate for 30 minutes.

2. Prepare and preheat a charcoal grill for indirect cooking, with one hot side and one hold (unheated) side. Adjust the grill vents to maintain a temperature of 225° to 250°F (see Controlling the Grill Temperature, page 17).

3. Remove the trout from the brine (discard the brine) and pat dry with paper towels. Place skin-side down on the hold side of the grill, cover the grill, and cook until flaky and cooked through, about 35 minutes.

4. Using 2 tablespoons of the olive oil, brush both sides of the bread slices, season with salt, and place on the grill. Cook until slightly charred and toasted on both sides, about 30 seconds per side.

5. Meanwhile, in a medium bowl, whisk together the lemon juice, remaining 6 tablespoons olive oil, and the capers. Season with a pinch of salt and twist of pepper. Add the arugula, onions, and dill and toss to combine.

6. Transfer the trout to a platter, top with the salad, and serve with grilled bread.

Quick Marinated Grilled Scallops

Serves 4

12 large (U10/U12) sea
scallops, side muscle
removed
½ cup extra-virgin olive oil,
plus more for drizzling
3 garlic cloves, minced
1 tablespoon finely chopped
fresh oregano
Grated zest and juice
of 2 lemons
Kosher salt and freshly
ground black pepper

Typically, if I'm making sea scallops, I'm searing them fast in
a ripping-hot pan. But this is a fun alternative way to prepare
them on the grill, where a quick citrusy marinade imparts bright,
tropical flavors. I've said it before and I'll say it again: Do not
overcook scallops or they will turn into bouncy Super Balls!
About two minutes per side on a hot grill should do the trick.

1. Place the scallops in a 1-gallon zip-top bag.

2. In a medium bowl, whisk together the olive oil, garlic, oregano,
   lemon zest, and lemon juice. Season with a pinch of salt and twist
   of pepper. Pour the marinade over the scallops and refrigerate for
   30 minutes.

3. Prepare and preheat a charcoal grill for direct cooking.

4. Remove the scallops from the bag, allowing most of the marinade
   to drip off (discard the marinade). Season the scallops with a
   pinch of salt and twist of pepper and drizzle with olive oil.

5. Place the scallops on the grill and cook until nicely charred and
   firm to the touch, about 2 minutes per side. Remove from the grill
   and serve.

Grill-Roasted Cauliflower
with Lime Vinaigrette
Serves 4

4 scallions, white and light-green parts only, thinly sliced (about ½ cup)

½ cup fresh cilantro leaves

¼ cup extra-virgin olive oil, plus more for drizzling

Grated zest and juice of 1 lime

1 teaspoon cumin seeds, toasted

1 small head white cauliflower, cut into florets (about 2 cups)

1 small head purple cauliflower, cut into florets (about 2 cups)

1 small head orange or green cauliflower, cut into florets (about 2 cups)

Kosher salt and freshly ground black pepper

Note: Toasting whole spices: Place a dry skillet over medium heat. Add the spices and heat until fragrant, stirring frequently until golden, about 3 minutes. Remove from the pan immediately.

As most of you know, I am definitely not a vegetarian. But man do I love veggies, especially when they are bursting with flavor, texture, and color like this amazing cauliflower dish. I call for a trio of varieties—white, purple, and orange—because I think it is impressive on the platter, but it's not a big deal if you can only find white cauliflower.

1. Prepare and preheat a charcoal grill for indirect cooking, with one hot side and one hold (unheated) side.

2. In a medium bowl, whisk together the scallions, cilantro, olive oil, lime zest, lime juice, and cumin. Set aside.

3. Place the cauliflower in a large bowl, drizzle with some olive oil, season with a pinch of salt and twist of pepper, and toss to coat.

4. Set a large cast-iron skillet on the hold side of the grill, add the cauliflower, cover the grill, and cook the cauliflower without moving until lightly charred and tender, about 20 minutes.

5. Transfer the cauliflower to a large bowl, add the lime vinaigrette, toss to coat, and serve.

Grilled Swordfish
with Salsa Fresca
Serves 4

4 boneless, skinless
swordfish steaks
(6 to 8 ounces each)
Extra-virgin olive oil, for
drizzling
Kosher salt and freshly
ground black pepper
1 large vine or heirloom
tomato, finely diced
(about 2 cups)
¼ cup finely chopped
red onion
¼ cup finely chopped
fresh cilantro
1 small jalapeño, seeded
and minced
1 teaspoon white wine
vinegar
Juice of 1 lime

Swordfish is made for the grill. It's firm, meaty, and typically sold as inch-thick steaks, making them easier to handle than, say, a tender fillet. I like to just drizzle them with oil and toss them on a hot grill until they are nice and charred on both sides. The fish will continue to cook a little off the grill, so don't overdo it on the time. For the perfect summer supper, just add a fresh Mexican-inspired salsa like this one and enjoy the evening.

1. Prepare and preheat a charcoal grill for direct cooking.

2. Drizzle both sides of the swordfish with some olive oil and season with a few pinches of salt and twists of pepper. Put the fish on the grill and cook until nicely charred and cooked through, about 3 minutes per side. Loosely tent with foil and set aside while you make the salsa.

3. In a medium bowl, stir together the tomato, onion, cilantro, jalapeño, vinegar, and lime juice. Season with a pinch of salt and twist of pepper.

4. Transfer the swordfish to a platter, top with salsa fresca, and any accumulated juices, and serve.

Gyro-Style Lamb Burgers
with Tzatziki and Grilled Onion

Serves 4

Tzatziki

1 cup whole-milk Greek
  yogurt
¼ cup finely chopped
  cucumber
1½ tablespoons finely
  chopped fresh dill
1 tablespoon finely chopped
  fresh mint
1 garlic clove, minced
Grated zest of ½ lemon
Kosher salt and freshly
  ground black pepper

Lamb Burgers

1½ pounds ground lamb
3 tablespoons finely
  chopped fresh mint
2 teaspoons ground
  coriander
Kosher salt and freshly
  ground black pepper

Assembly

1 large red onion, sliced into
  1-inch-thick rings
Extra-virgin olive oil, for
  drizzling
Kosher salt and freshly
  ground black pepper
4 pita breads, split
2 medium vine or heirloom
  tomatoes, diced
½ head romaine lettuce,
  cored and roughly
  chopped

Every single time I make a lamb dish, the famous scene from *My Big Fat Greek Wedding* pops into my head. After Toula explains to her aunt that her boyfriend Ian is a vegetarian, her aunt says, "That's okay, I make him lamb!" Not quite "the other white meat," but lamb definitely deserves a more prominent place in people's diets, I think. It has so much flavor and is extremely versatile. Even if it's just the occasional gyro—or in this case, gyro-style burger—people should be stepping up to lamb.

1. Prepare and preheat a charcoal grill for direct cooking.

2. Make the tzatziki: In a medium bowl, stir together the yogurt, cucumber, dill, mint, garlic, and lemon zest. Season with a pinch of salt and twist of pepper. Refrigerate until needed.

3. Make the lamb burgers: In a medium bowl, mix together the lamb, mint, and coriander. Using your hands, form the meat into 4 patties. Season with a pinch of salt and twist of pepper. Place the patties on the grill and cook until the burgers are golden brown and crisp on the edges, about 4 minutes per side.

4. Meanwhile, to assemble: Drizzle the onion rings with olive oil and season with a few pinches of salt and twists of pepper. Put on the grill and cook, flipping the onions halfway, until nicely charred, about 10 minutes total.

5. Place the burgers in the pitas, top with the tzatziki, grilled onion, tomato, and lettuce and serve.

Skillet-Grilled Chicken Piccata

Serves 4

4 boneless, skinless chicken breasts (6 ounces each)

Kosher salt and freshly ground black pepper

2 tablespoons extra-virgin olive oil

2 tablespoons unsalted butter

4 garlic cloves, sliced

¾ cup dry white wine

¾ cup chicken stock

2 tablespoons capers, rinsed

Juice of 1 lemon

2 tablespoons finely chopped fresh flat-leaf parsley

Here is another classic Italian American recipe that I adapted for the grill. This version manages to pack in the bold, bright, tantalizing flavors of the timeless favorite but accomplishes it in half the time and all outdoors. For this easy-breezy prep, we skip the bothersome pounding of the chicken breasts and even the dredging in flour. But we certainly don't leave out the silky-smooth sauce enriched with butter and finished with plenty of lemon, capers, and parsley. The natural side dish choice here is the Grill-Roasted Garlic Bread (page 76), but you can also go with a simple salad and some pasta.

1. Prepare and preheat a charcoal grill for direct cooking.

2. Season the chicken on all sides with salt and pepper. Set a large cast-iron skillet on the grill. Add the olive oil and 1 tablespoon of the butter and heat to shimmering. Add the chicken and cook until golden brown on both sides, about 3 minutes per side. Transfer to a plate.

3. To the same skillet, add ½ tablespoon of the butter, the garlic, and a pinch of salt. Cook, stirring occasionally, until aromatic, about 2 minutes. Add the wine and cook until slightly reduced, about 1 minute. Add the chicken stock and bring to a simmer.

4. Return the chicken to the skillet and cook until the meat reaches an internal temperature of 165°F, about 5 minutes.

5. Remove the skillet from the heat, add the capers, lemon juice, parsley, and remaining ½ tablespoon butter and stir to combine.

6. Plate the chicken, spoon over some sauce, and serve.

Grilled Chicken Souvlaki

Serves 6 to 8

3 pounds boneless, skinless chicken thighs, cut into 1-inch pieces

6 tablespoons extra-virgin olive oil

6 tablespoons red wine vinegar

2 garlic cloves, minced

3 tablespoons finely chopped fresh oregano

Grated zest and juice of 2 lemons

1 tablespoon Diamond Crystal kosher salt

Is it just me or does food always taste better when it's put on a skewer and grilled? My parents would make souvlaki with pork, beef, lamb, or chicken—didn't matter which one, we always devoured them. This recipe would work great with any of those proteins, by the way. The key is to let the marinade do its job for at least a couple hours—preferably overnight—and to get a really nice char from the grill. I like to serve this with a Crispy Pita Salad (page 31) and/or Duck Fat–Fried Potatoes (page 78).

1. Place the chicken in a 1-gallon zip-top bag.

2. In a large bowl, whisk together the olive oil, vinegar, garlic, oregano, lemon zest, and lemon juice. Pour the marinade over the chicken and refrigerate for at least 4 hours or up to overnight.

3. Prepare and preheat a charcoal grill for indirect cooking, with one hot side and one hold (unheated) side.

4. Set eight 10-inch skewers on a work surface (if using wood skewers, soak them in a shallow dish of water for at least 30 minutes). Remove the chicken from the bag, allowing most of the marinade to drip off (discard the marinade). Thread 4 or 5 pieces of meat onto each of the skewers, grouping them near the top so that the tip is covered by the meat, but leaving space to grab the skewer at the bottom.

5. Season on all sides with the salt and put on the hot side of the grill. Cook until lightly charred on all sides, about 6 minutes per side. Move the skewers to the hold side of the grill, cover the grill, and cook until the meat reaches an internal temperature of 165°F, about 10 minutes.

City Chicken Skewers

Serves 4

2 pounds pork tenderloin,
  trimmed of its silver skin,
  cut into 2-inch cubes
Kosher salt and freshly
  ground black pepper
½ cup all-purpose flour
2 large eggs
2 cups plain dried bread
  crumbs
1 teaspoon sweet paprika
1 tablespoon extra-virgin
  olive oil

Here's a little secret: I didn't discover until later in life that the "city chicken" we ate growing up wasn't, ahem, chicken. If you grew up in Cleveland when I did, you probably ate this dish. If you grew up anywhere else, however, the notion probably sounds insane. The act of substituting pork (or veal) for chicken originated during the Depression, when poultry was more expensive than pork. After cubing, skewering, breading, and frying the meat, who could even tell what it was?! It might have humble origins, but the dish still makes me smile. I like to serve these with Grill-Roasted Tomatoes with Herby Bread Crumbs (page 88) or Grilled Radicchio with Buttermilk Dressing (page 62).

1. Prepare and preheat a charcoal grill for indirect cooking, with one hot side and one hold (unheated) side.

2. Set eight 8-inch skewers on a work surface (if using wooden skewers, soak them in a shallow dish of water for at least 30 minutes). Thread 5 or 6 pieces of pork onto each skewer. Season all sides of the pork with a few pinches of salt and twists of black pepper.

3. Set a large cast-iron skillet on the hot side of the grill.

4. Set up a dredging station in three shallow bowls: Put the flour in one bowl. Lightly beat the eggs with 2 tablespoons water in a second bowl. Mix together the bread crumbs and paprika in the third bowl. Working with one skewer at a time, dredge the pork in the flour, making sure to coat all sides well. Shake off the excess. Dip the pork into the beaten eggs, allowing the excess to drip off. Finally, lay the pork in the bread crumbs, turning and pressing to fully coat all sides.

5. Add the olive oil to the preheated skillet, followed by the pork skewers. Cook, without moving, until nicely browned on all sides, about 3 minutes per side. Slide the skillet to the hold side, cover the grill, and cook until the meat reaches an internal temperature of 150°F, about 15 minutes.

6. Plate the skewers and serve.

4

Feed a Crowd

Just like the name says, these are some of my go-to dishes that I lean on when cooking for a big crew. Whether it's football Sunday, a posh birthday brunch, or just a glorious summer night to savor with friends, the recipes in this chapter are either plentiful enough to feed a crowd or designed to easily scale up to do so.

Obviously, hearty favorites like Beef and Potato Casserole (page 138) and Mom's American Dish (page 160) instantly come to mind, but so do boldly flavored pasta dishes like Clams with Sausage and Peppers (page 168) and Cavatelli with Sausage and Broccoli Rabe (page 163). For tailgating with friends, it's impossible to outdo the Birria-Style Beef Tacos (page 165), especially when paired with a few ice-cold beers. And for an easy but tasteful weeknight supper, the citrusy Spatchcock Chicken (page 147) is my number-one choice.

Meatball Parmesan Sandwiches

Serves 4

1½ pounds ground beef (80% lean)

1 cup whole-milk ricotta cheese

½ cup whole milk

½ cup freshly grated parmesan cheese

¾ cup dried bread crumbs

½ cup finely chopped fresh flat-leaf parsley

1 medium yellow onion, finely chopped (about 1 cup)

1 large egg

4 garlic cloves, minced

½ teaspoon freshly grated nutmeg

Kosher salt and freshly ground black pepper

2 tablespoons extra-virgin olive oil

1 tablespoon finely chopped fresh oregano

1 (28-ounce) can tomato puree

4 sandwich rolls, split

1 (8-ounce) ball fresh mozzarella, sliced

½ cup torn fresh basil leaves

If a meatball sub and chicken parmesan had a love child, it would be this amazing hoagie! What's not to love about flavorful homemade meatballs smothered in red sauce, capped with fresh mozz, and finished with bright, fresh basil? You're not likely to stumble upon this stick-to-your-ribs sandwich in Italy, but that doesn't mean it's not delicious!

1. Prepare and preheat a charcoal grill for indirect cooking, with one hot side and one hold (unheated) side.

2. In a large bowl, combine the beef, ricotta, milk, parmesan, bread crumbs, parsley, half the chopped onion, the egg, half the minced garlic, and the nutmeg. Season with a few pinches of salt and twists of pepper. Mix to combine, being careful not to overwork the mixture. Using your hands, divide the mixture into 8 equal portions and form into meatballs slightly larger than a golf ball.

3. Set a large nonreactive skillet on the grill. Add the olive oil and heat to shimmering. Add the meatballs and cook, without disturbing, until golden brown, about 3 minutes. Continue browning on the other sides, about 3 minutes per side. Add the remaining onions, remaining garlic, and oregano and cook, stirring occasionally, until the vegetables begin to soften, about 3 minutes. Stir in the tomato puree and ½ cup water. Move the pan to the hold side of the grill, cover the grill, and cook until the sauce reduces by one-quarter, about 10 minutes.

4. Place the sandwich rolls on the hot side of the grill cut-side down and toast until golden brown, about 1 minute.

5. Divide the meatballs among the rolls, spoon over some sauce, and top with sliced mozzarella. Set the sandwiches on the hold side of the grill, cover the grill, and cook until the cheese is melted, about 5 minutes. Top with basil and serve.

Beef and Potato Casserole

Serves 6

1 cup shredded cheddar cheese

2 tablespoons cornstarch

6 tablespoons extra-virgin olive oil

2 pounds ground beef (80% lean)

1 large yellow onion, diced (about 1 cup)

2 tablespoons finely chopped fresh thyme

1 garlic clove, minced

Kosher salt and freshly ground black pepper

½ cup all-purpose flour

3 large russet potatoes, peeled and medium diced

2 tablespoons canned chipotle puree

1 tablespoon sweet paprika

4 cups whole milk

1½ cups panko bread crumbs

1 cup freshly grated parmesan cheese

8 scallions, white and light-green parts only, thinly sliced (about 1 cup)

If your family loves steak and potatoes, this is a delicious—and inexpensive—way to satisfy those cravings. Although it looks like a ton of ingredients, it's all pretty basic stuff, and the whole thing comes together in under an hour (and for most of that time you're coasting). This hearty, cheesy casserole will stay hot for close to 45 minutes and the leftovers are just as good as the day you made it.

1. Prepare and preheat a charcoal grill for indirect cooking, with one hot side and one hold (unheated) side. Adjust the grill vents to maintain a temperature of 350° to 375°F (see Controlling the Grill Temperature, page 17).

2. In a medium bowl, toss together the cheddar and cornstarch.

3. Place a 9 × 13-inch metal baking pan or grill-safe ceramic baking dish on the hot side of the grill. Add the olive oil and heat to shimmering. Add the beef, onions, thyme, and garlic. Season with a pinch of salt and twist of pepper. Cook, stirring with a wooden spoon to break up the meat, until lightly browned, about 5 minutes. Add the flour and cook, while stirring, for 2 minutes. Add the potatoes, chipotle puree, and paprika and stir to combine. While continuously whisking, slowly add the milk. Bring the mixture up to a simmer and then move to the hold side of the grill. Taste and adjust for seasoning, adding salt and pepper as needed.

4. Add the cheddar and cornstarch mixture and whisk until the cheese has melted. Top with the panko and parmesan. Cover the grill and cook until golden brown and the potatoes are tender, about 40 minutes.

5. Remove from the grill, top with scallions, and serve.

Coney Dogs

Serves 8

Chili

1 tablespoon extra-virgin olive oil

1 pound ground beef (80% lean)

½ pound ground beef heart (optional; if not using, bump up the ground beef to 1½ pounds)

1 teaspoon Diamond Crystal kosher salt

½ teaspoon freshly ground black pepper

1½ cups diced yellow onion (about 1½ medium onions)

1 medium red bell pepper, diced (about 1 cup)

2 garlic cloves, minced

4 teaspoons chipotle powder

1 teaspoon sweet paprika

1 teaspoon ground cumin

1 teaspoon dried oregano

⅛ teaspoon ground cloves

2 tablespoons apple cider vinegar

½ cup tomato paste

3 tablespoons all-purpose flour

1½ cups beef stock

Coneys

8 natural-casing beef hot dogs

8 hot dog buns

Yellow mustard, for serving

½ cup diced white onion (about ½ medium)

Hot sauce, for serving

Long before I opened Roast in Detroit, my father worked for Ford, so we traveled to the Motor City as a family frequently. No visit was complete without a trip to American or Lafayette, two spots famous for coneys, those massively craveable meat sauce–topped hot dogs. While the original recipes have been cloaked in mystery, secrecy, and confusion for decades, it's pretty common knowledge that beef hearts were used in place of some or all of the ground beef, which is both economical and supremely beefy in flavor. Most good butcher shops can hook you up. I prefer a ratio of two parts ground beef to one part ground heart, but this will still be great if you omit the heart. At home, I serve these with yellow mustard, chopped onion, and hot sauce. My granddaughter Emmy loves them, beef heart and all!

1. Prepare and preheat a charcoal grill for indirect cooking, with one hot side and one hold (unheated) side.

2. Make the chili: Set a large enameled Dutch oven on the hot side of the grill. Add the olive oil and heat to shimmering. Add the ground beef, beef heart (if using), salt, and black pepper. Cook, stirring with a wooden spoon to break up the meat, until lightly browned, about 5 minutes.

3. Add the onion, bell pepper, and garlic and cook, stirring occasionally, for 1 minute. Add the chipotle powder, paprika, cumin, oregano, cloves, and vinegar and cook, stirring constantly, until aromatic, about 30 seconds. Add the tomato paste and flour and cook, stirring occasionally, until the paste begins to darken, about 2 minutes. Add the stock and deglaze the pan, scraping with a wooden spoon to get up the browned bits on the bottom of the pan. Bring to a simmer, move to the hold side of the grill, and partially cover the pot. Cover the grill and cook, stirring occasionally, until the chili is nice and thick and the flavors have come together, about 2 hours. Top off the charcoal as needed (see Replenishing Briquettes, page 15).

4. When the chili is ready, assemble the coneys: Put the hot dogs on the grill and cook until golden brown and crispy, about 3 minutes per side. At the same time, put the buns on the hold side of the grill to warm.

5. Place the hot dogs in the buns, top with mustard, chili, and diced onion. Serve with hot sauce on the side.

Symon's Juicy Lucy
Double Cheese and Bacon Burger

Serves 4

¼ cup mayonnaise (Duke's or Hellmann's)

¼ cup hot or Dijon mustard

2 tablespoons barbecue sauce

1½ pounds ground beef (80% lean)

4 thick slices cheddar cheese, quartered

4 slices bacon, small diced

Kosher salt and freshly ground black pepper

4 potato rolls

1 small red onion, halved and thinly sliced (about ½ cup)

Pickle slices, for serving

Mustard, for serving (I like POP Smoked Whole Seed)

This over-the-top creation is an ode to the Juicy Lucy, a cheese-stuffed burger made famous by a few now-iconic Minneapolis burger joints. Why put cheese on top of the patty when you can tuck it inside? At least, that was the belief at places like Matt's Bar & Grill and the 5-8 Club, both of which lay claim to the first juicy, cheese-dripping iterations. When it comes to variations, the sky's the limit, but I love using sharp cheddar cheese inside, pickles and raw onion underneath, pressing chopped bacon into the top of the patty *before* cooking, and finishing with a simple BBQ-spiked "special" sauce on both sides of the bun.

1. Prepare and preheat a charcoal grill for indirect cooking, with one hot side and one hold (unheated) side.

2. In a medium bowl, whisk together the mayonnaise, hot mustard, and barbecue sauce. Set aside until needed.

3. Set a large cast-iron skillet on the hot side of the grill to preheat.

4. Divide the beef into 8 equal portions and form into patties 2 inches thick. Working with 1 patty at a time, place 4 quarters of cheddar in the center of the patty, top with a second patty, and press to join and seal the meat. Repeat with the remaining patties and cheese. Top each patty with one-quarter of the chopped bacon, pressing it into the beef so it stays in place. Season the burgers with a pinch of salt and twist of pepper.

5. Set 2 patties bacon-side down in the skillet. Using a heavy metal spatula, lightly press each patty. Cook until the bacon is golden brown and crisp, about 5 minutes. Spread 1 tablespoon of the prepared sauce on top of the burgers, flip the burgers sauce-side down, and cook until the second side is golden brown, about 3 minutes. Move the burgers to the hold side of the grill while you repeat the process with the remaining burgers.

6. Spread some of the remaining sauce on the tops and bottoms of the rolls. Divide the onion slices among the bottom halves, add a few pickle slices, top with burgers, mustard, and then the top buns, and serve.

Eggs in Heaven

Serves 4

3 tablespoons unsalted butter

1 small yellow onion, diced (about ½ cup)

1 medium red bell pepper, diced (about 1 cup)

Kosher salt

3 tablespoons all-purpose flour

2 cups whole milk

1 cup grated cheddar cheese

4 ounces cream cheese, at room temperature

1 cup diced ham

½ teaspoon red pepper flakes

½ teaspoon freshly grated nutmeg

Freshly ground black pepper

8 large eggs

As the name suggests, this recipe is the antithesis to eggs in hell (also known as eggs in purgatory). Whereas the latter refers to eggs poached in a diabolically spicy tomato sauce, this dish goes in a completely different direction. Here, eggs are baked in a creamy and decadent white sauce enriched with cream cheese and studded with bits of salty ham. When you pop the yolks, that sauce takes on a golden hue that looks, dare I say, heavenly!

1. Prepare and preheat a charcoal grill for indirect cooking, with one hot side and one hold (unheated) side. Adjust the grill vents to maintain a temperature of 350°F (see Controlling the Grill Temperature, page 17).

2. Set a large cast-iron skillet on the hot side of the grill. Add the butter and allow to melt, then add the onion, bell pepper, and a pinch of salt. Cook, stirring occasionally, until the vegetables begin to soften, about 3 minutes. Add the flour and cook, while stirring, for 1 minute. While continuously whisking, slowly add the milk. Cook, uncovered, stirring frequently, until reduced by one-third, about 20 minutes.

3. Remove from the heat, add the cheddar and cream cheese and whisk until the cheeses have melted. Add the ham, pepper flakes, and nutmeg and stir to combine. Season with a pinch of salt and twist of pepper. Carefully crack the eggs into the sauce, leaving space between them. Place the skillet on the hold side, cover the grill, and cook until the egg whites are set but the yolks are still runny, about 10 minutes.

4. Serve immediately.

Stuffed Tomatoes

Serves 4

4 large beefsteak tomatoes

Kosher salt and freshly ground black pepper

2 tablespoons extra-virgin olive oil, plus more for drizzling

½ pound ground beef (80% lean)

1 small yellow onion, diced (about ½ cup)

2 garlic cloves, minced

1½ cups cooked long-grain rice

4 ounces crumbled fresh goat cheese (about ¾ cup)

½ cup finely chopped fresh flat-leaf parsley

¼ cup pine nuts

2 tablespoons finely chopped fresh mint

Grated zest of 1 lemon

2 tablespoons panko bread crumbs

You'd think that I was on the board of the Tomato Growers Association by all the tomato-themed recipes in this book, but I can't help it! Growing up, we had an endless supply of juicy, vine-ripened tomatoes coming out of the family garden, so we learned to appreciate variety. And for most of us, cooking outside overlaps tomato season, so it just makes sense. Many kids hate cooked tomatoes, but I always thought cooking made them sweeter and more delicious. Especially Mom's famous stuffed tomatoes, filled with seasoned ground beef, rice, pine nuts, and herbs. The only way to make it better, I have found, is to prepare it on the grill, where it takes on a little kiss of smoke.

1. Prepare and preheat a charcoal grill for indirect cooking, with one hot side and one hold (unheated) side.

2. Slice ½ inch off the top of the tomatoes and use a spoon to scoop out the pulp and seeds. Roughly chop the scooped-out tomato pulp and set it aside. Season the insides of the tomatoes with a few pinches of salt and twists of pepper.

3. Set a large skillet on the hot side of the grill. Add the olive oil and heat to shimmering. Add the ground beef and cook, stirring with a wooden spoon to break up the meat, until lightly browned, about 5 minutes. Add the onion, garlic, and a pinch of salt and cook, stirring occasionally, until aromatic, about 1 minute. Add the reserved chopped tomato and cook, scraping with a wooden spoon to get up the browned bits on the bottom of the pan, for 1 minute. Remove the skillet from the heat and stir in the rice, goat cheese, parsley, pine nuts, mint, and lemon zest. Transfer to a bowl.

4. Place the tomatoes in the skillet, fill them to the top with the beef mixture, top with the panko, and drizzle with some olive oil. Place on the hold side of the grill, cover the grill, and cook until the tops are golden brown, about 20 minutes.

5. Drizzle with more olive oil and serve.

Spatchcock Chicken

Serves 4

1 whole chicken
(3 to 4 pounds)
Grated zest and juice
of 2 oranges
¼ cup extra-virgin olive oil,
plus more for drizzling
1 tablespoon fresh oregano
leaves
1 teaspoon sweet paprika
Kosher salt and freshly
ground black pepper

I like to make spatchcock chickens because I like to say the word "spatchcock." (I know, I need to grow up!) In all seriousness, this is the best way to grill a whole chicken. By removing the backbone and flattening out the bird, you accomplish a few key things. First, you get better skin- and meat-to-grill contact, which creates that all-important char and crust. But perhaps even more important, the white and dark meat cook more evenly, resulting in juicier white meat. And as an added bonus, the process drastically reduces cooking time. Serve this with a big, beautiful salad, some crusty sourdough, and a great bottle of white wine.

1. Place the chicken breast-side down on a cutting board and, using heavy-duty kitchen shears, cut along both sides of the backbone and remove it. Discard the backbone (or save it for stock). Flip the chicken and open it up so it lies somewhat flat on the cutting board, skin-side up. Use your palm to press and crack the breastbone so the chicken lies flatter.

2. In a large bowl, whisk together the orange zest, orange juice, olive oil, oregano, and paprika. Season with a pinch of salt and twist of pepper. Add the chicken and coat all sides with the marinade. Cover and refrigerate for at least 2 hours and up to 6 hours.

3. Prepare and preheat a charcoal grill for indirect cooking, with one hot side and one hold (unheated) side.

4. Remove the chicken from the marinade, allowing the excess to drip off (discard the marinade). Drizzle the chicken on both sides with some olive oil and season with a few pinches of salt and twists of pepper.

5. Place the chicken skin-side down on the hot side of the grill and cook until nicely charred, about 5 minutes. Flip the chicken and move it to the hold side of the grill. Cover the grill and cook until the meat reaches an internal temperature of 160°F at the leg/thigh joint, about 45 minutes.

6. Let rest for 15 minutes before cutting into 4 pieces and serving.

Crispy Feta Eggs

Serves 4

1 large beefsteak tomato, diced

1 avocado, diced

½ cup plus 3 tablespoons extra-virgin olive oil

3 scallions, white and light-green parts only, thinly sliced (about ⅓ cup)

¼ cup pitted Niçoise olives, sliced

¼ cup red wine vinegar

2 tablespoons finely chopped fresh oregano

Kosher salt and freshly ground black pepper

4 pita breads

1 cup crumbled Greek feta cheese

8 large eggs

If I could always start my day with this Greek-style breakfast I would be a happy man. It combines cheese-fried eggs with a bright tomato and olive salad. Warm pita is served on the side to scoop up the runny yolks. Until you've tried eggs fried on top of crispy melted feta, you haven't lived!

1. Prepare and preheat a charcoal grill for indirect cooking, with one hot side and one hold (unheated) side.

2. In a large bowl, combine the tomato, avocado, ½ cup of the olive oil, the scallions, olives, vinegar, and oregano. Season with a pinch of salt and twist of pepper and toss to combine.

3. Set a large cast-iron skillet on the hot side of the grill to heat for 1 minute. Wrap the pita in foil.

4. Add the remaining 3 tablespoons olive oil to the skillet and heat to shimmering. Scatter the feta evenly across the bottom of the skillet and cook, without stirring, for 1 minute, until slightly melted and lightly crisp on the edges. Crack the eggs into the skillet and cook, without stirring, until a crust begins to form, about 2 minutes. Place the pita on the hold side of the grill. Cover the grill and cook for 1 minute, until the whites are set and the yolks are slightly runny.

5. Remove the skillet and the pita bread from the grill. Transfer the eggs to a platter, top with the tomato salad, and serve with warm pita.

Slow-Grilled Pork Butt Steaks
with Cherry BBQ Sauce

Serves 4

Pork

- 1 tablespoon Diamond Crystal kosher salt
- 1 tablespoon sugar
- 2 teaspoons onion powder
- 2 teaspoons garlic powder
- 1 teaspoons red pepper flakes
- 4 pork butt steaks (aka pork shoulder steaks), 1¼ inches thick

Cherry BBQ Sauce

- 2 tablespoons extra-virgin olive oil
- 1 small yellow onion, diced (about ½ cup)
- 1 jalapeño, seeded and diced
- Kosher salt
- 1 teaspoon ground cumin
- 1 teaspoon ground coriander
- 2 cups pitted cherries, fresh or frozen
- 1 (7.5-ounce) can Dr Pepper
- ¼ cup molasses
- 1 tablespoon Worcestershire sauce
- Freshly ground black pepper
- Juice of ½ lemon
- 1 tablespoon balsamic vinegar

Pork butt steaks, which are actually cut from the shoulder, are well marbled and extremely flavorful. While they can be cooked over a hot grill just like a beef steak, I prefer to cook them low and slow over indirect heat. Not only do they pick up a ton more flavor from the smoke, I think the process results in a much juicier and more tender finished product. The steaks get finished on the grill with a sweet and fruity BBQ sauce (secret ingredient? Cherries and Dr Pepper!), which gets cooked into the meat. You can think of these as your gateway to barbecue; once you master these pork steaks you can move on up to a whole pork butt, and then, brisket! Note that after rubbing with spices, the steaks have to dry marinate for at least 3 hours or overnight.

1. Dry marinate the pork: In a small bowl, whisk together the salt, sugar, onion powder, garlic powder, and pepper flakes. Season the pork steaks liberally on both sides with the rub, cover, and refrigerate for at least 3 hours and up to overnight.

2. Prepare and preheat a charcoal grill for indirect cooking, with one hot side and one hold (unheated) side. Adjust the grill vents to maintain a temperature of 250° to 275°F (see Controlling the Grill Temperature, page 17).

3. Make the cherry BBQ sauce: Set a medium saucepan on the hot side of the grill. Add the olive oil and heat to shimmering. Add the onion, jalapeño, and a pinch of salt. Cook, stirring occasionally, until the vegetables soften, about 3 minutes. Add the cumin and coriander and cook, stirring occasionally, for 1 minute, until aromatic. Add the cherries, Dr Pepper, molasses, and Worcestershire and whisk to combine. Season with a few pinches of salt and twists of pepper. Bring to a gentle simmer and cook, stirring occasionally, until the cherries soften and the flavors come together, about 15 minutes.

4. Carefully transfer the sauce to a blender or food processor and puree until smooth. (If using a blender, pulse briefly at first and open the steam vent in the lid to ensure the contents don't explode!) Stir in the lemon juice and vinegar and set aside.

recipe continues

5. When the temperature in the grill reaches 250° to 275°F, put the pork steaks on the hold side of the grill. Cover the grill and cook for 1½ hours. Top off the charcoal as needed (see Replenishing Briquettes, page 15).

6. Flip the steaks and cook until the meat reaches an internal temperature of 165°F, about 30 minutes. During the last 30 minutes of cooking, baste the meat with BBQ sauce every 10 minutes.

7. Transfer the steaks to a platter and let rest for 10 minutes before serving with the remaining BBQ sauce on the side.

Pastrami-Smoked Pork Belly

Serves 8

½ cup kosher salt
½ cup coarsely ground
　black pepper
¼ cup celery seeds
¼ cup ground coriander
2 tablespoons garlic powder
2 tablespoons coarsely
　cracked mustard seeds
2 tablespoons sweet
　paprika
1 skin-off pork belly (10 to
　12 pounds)
1 cup yellow mustard
Apple cider, for spraying
Whole-seed mustard,
　for serving (I like POP
　Mustard)

Pork belly is one of my all-time favorite ingredients. Cured and smoked, it becomes bacon, of course. But there are so many other ways to prepare this versatile—and forgiving—piece of meat. In winter, I like to slow-roast it in the oven, where it cooks in its own fat and becomes insanely juicy, tender, and sweet. In summer, I'll even grill thick-sliced pork belly by quickly searing it over high heat and then sliding the meat over to the hold side to finish. But my favorite way to cook pork belly is to give it a good spice rub and smoke it, low and slow, until it's melt-in-your-mouth piggy pudding. Grab yourself a clean spray bottle, fill it with apple cider, and spritz the meat every half hour or so during cooking. It helps to tenderize the meat, enhances crust development, and maintains moisture. Serve this with a good-quality whole-seed mustard like POP Mustard.

1. Prepare and preheat a charcoal grill for indirect cooking using the snake method or the minion method to maintain a temperature of 250° to 275°F (see Controlling the Grill Temperature, page 17).

2. In a small bowl, whisk together the salt, pepper, celery seeds, coriander, garlic powder, mustard seeds, and paprika. Pat the pork belly dry with paper towels, coat with the yellow mustard, then season on all sides with the spice rub.

3. Put the pork belly on the hold side of the grill, cover the grill, and cook until the meat reaches an internal temperature of 185°F, about 2½ hours. If not using the snake or minion method, top off the charcoal as needed. For the best results, use a probe thermometer to continually monitor the meat's temperature. After the first hour of cooking, spray the pork belly with apple cider every 30 minutes.

4. Transfer the meat to a cutting board, cover with foil, and let rest for 30 minutes. Slice to the desired thickness and serve with whole-seed mustard.

Fettuccine
with Smoked Tomato Sauce
Serves 4

3 pounds plum tomatoes, quartered

1 large red onion, thickly sliced

8 garlic cloves, thinly sliced

Grated zest and juice of 1 lime

1 tablespoon cumin seeds

1 tablespoon Diamond Crystal kosher salt

1 tablespoon extra-virgin olive oil

1 pound fettuccine, cooked

Freshly grated parmesan cheese, for serving

This is my standard tomato sauce for pasta, but here, I lightly smoke the tomatoes and vegetables first, which gives the sauce incredible depth. It's not super-smoky like a campfire; it's just a kiss. If you want to bump up the smoky factor, toss a few chunks of oak or cherrywood onto the hot coals when you add the tomatoes. Use this on pasta as I do here or substitute it for regular tomato sauce in recipes, such as chicken parm, lasagna, or baked ziti, to give the dish a special touch.

1. Prepare and preheat a charcoal grill for indirect cooking, with one hot side and one hold (unheated) side. Adjust the grill vents to maintain a temperature of 225°F (see Controlling the Grill Temperature, page 17).

2. In a large bowl, toss together the tomatoes, onion, garlic, lime zest, lime juice, cumin, salt, and olive oil. Transfer to a sheet pan.

3. Place the vegetables on the hold side of the grill and cook for 1 hour. Top off the charcoal as needed (see Replenishing Briquettes, page 15).

4. Carefully transfer the smoked vegetables and any accumulated juices to a blender or food processor and process until smooth. (If using a blender, pulse briefly at first and open the steam vent in the lid to ensure the contents don't explode!)

5. Pour the sauce into a large skillet, set on the hot side of the grill, and cook until reduced by one-quarter, about 3 minutes.

6. Remove the sauce from the grill, add the cooked pasta, and stir to combine. Transfer the pasta to a serving bowl, garnish with parmesan, and serve.

Grilled Eggplant Parmesan

Serves 4

⅓ cup extra-virgin olive oil, plus more for drizzling

3 garlic cloves, grated

2 teaspoons finely chopped fresh oregano

2 medium eggplants, cut into ½-inch-thick rounds

Kosher salt and freshly ground black pepper

4 beefsteak tomatoes, cut into ½-inch-thick slices

8 ounces fresh mozzarella cheese, sliced

Fresh basil leaves, for serving

If you love the taste of eggplant parmesan but don't feel like slaving away in a hot kitchen, this recipe is for you. Not conventional by a long shot, this preparation swaps the oven for the grill, while also doing away with the breading, frying, layering, and long bake times. The finished product, though done in a fraction of the time, tastes like a freshened version of the original. I'm always looking for new and tasty ways to use eggplant, because I love it, and this is one of my summertime faves.

1. Prepare and preheat a charcoal grill for indirect cooking, with one hot side and one hold (unheated) side.

2. In a large bowl, stir together the olive oil, garlic, and oregano. Add the eggplant slices and toss to coat. Season with a few pinches of salt and twists of pepper. Put the eggplant slices on the hot side of the grill and cook until nicely charred and beginning to soften, about 3 minutes per side. If you don't have room to grill all the eggplant at once, work in batches, moving the cooked eggplant to the hold side to keep warm while you finish.

3. When all the eggplant is on the hold side, evenly distribute the tomato and mozzarella slices on top of each piece. Cover the grill and cook until the tomato has warmed through and the cheese has melted, about 4 minutes.

4. Transfer to a platter, drizzle with some olive oil, garnish with basil, and serve.

Mom's American Dish

Serves 4

2 tablespoons extra-virgin olive oil

1 pound ground beef (80% lean), pork, or lamb

Kosher salt and freshly ground black pepper

1 medium yellow onion, finely chopped

3 garlic cloves, minced

2 tablespoons finely chopped fresh oregano

1 (28-ounce) can crushed tomatoes

2 tablespoons tomato paste

1 pound cavatappi or elbow macaroni, cooked, ½ cup pasta water reserved

¼ cup crumbled feta cheese

We enjoyed a steady stream of hearty stews, casseroles, and goulashes at the Symon house—and you won't get any complaints from this guy. I love the comforting (and filling) combination of pasta, ground meat, and cheese. This one takes on a Greek flair thanks to the fresh oregano and feta, but my parents made so many variations over the years. And so do I, because few foods come together this quickly, for so little money, and offer such big rewards.

1. Prepare and preheat a charcoal grill for indirect cooking, with one hot side and one hold (unheated) side.

2. Set a large pot on the hot side of the grill. Add the olive oil and heat to shimmering. Add the ground beef, season with a pinch of salt and twist of pepper, and cook, stirring with a wooden spoon to break up the meat, until lightly browned, about 5 minutes.

3. Add the onion, garlic, and oregano and cook, stirring occasionally, until the onion softens and begins to brown, about 5 minutes.

4. Add the crushed tomatoes and tomato paste, season with salt and pepper, and bring to a simmer. Add the drained pasta and reserved pasta water and continue cooking, stirring occasionally, until slightly thickened, about 5 minutes.

5. Remove from the heat, stir in the feta, and serve.

Cavatelli
with Sausage and Broccoli Rabe
Serves 4

Ricotta Cavatelli

2 cups whole-milk ricotta
cheese

3 large eggs

½ teaspoon kosher salt

3 cups all-purpose flour,
plus more for rolling

Broccoli Rabe and Sausage

Kosher salt

2 pounds broccoli rabe,
woody stems trimmed

1 tablespoon extra-virgin
olive oil, plus more for
drizzling

1 pound loose sweet Italian
pork sausage

1 pound loose hot Italian
pork sausage

12 garlic cloves, sliced

2 teaspoons red pepper
flakes (optional)

½ cup freshly grated
pecorino cheese, plus
more for serving

Freshly ground black pepper

Growing up, our Sundays culminated in a big, boisterous family
meal starring slow-cooked sauce and, if we were lucky, tender
ricotta-enriched cavatelli. I have many fond memories of rolling
those out by hand on a flour-dusted table. In this alfresco
kitchen version, I pair the delicate cavatelli with a robust medley
of sausages, blanched rapini (aka broccoli rabe), and pecorino
cheese. It's a sweet, spicy, and slightly bitter dish that satisfies in
a big way.

1. Make the cavatelli: In a large bowl, combine the ricotta, eggs,
   and salt and stir to combine. Add the flour and mix by hand until
   the dough comes together into a ball. Add additional flour if the
   dough feels too sticky. Wrap in plastic and refrigerate for at least
   1 hour and up to overnight.

2. Lightly flour a work surface and sheet pan. Turn the dough out
   onto the floured surface and knead it into a round. With a bench
   scraper or knife, cut the dough into quarters. Using your palms
   and fingers, gently roll each piece out to a rope ¼ inch thick,
   adding flour when needed to prevent sticking. Cut each rope
   crosswise into ½-inch pieces. With a bench knife or table knife,
   gently press down on each piece, beginning at the top and
   moving down toward the bottom, dragging the knife toward you
   and causing the pasta to roll over onto itself. Transfer the formed
   pasta to the floured sheet pan and let dry at room temperature for
   at least 30 minutes and up to 1 hour. (The pasta can be frozen at
   this point for up to 1 month, if desired.)

3. Prepare and preheat a charcoal grill for indirect cooking, with
   one hot side and one hold (unheated) side.

4. Prepare the broccoli rabe and sausages: Add 2 tablespoons salt
   to a medium pot of water and bring to a boil on the hot side of
   the grill. Set up an ice bath by filling a large bowl with ice and
   water. Once the water is at a boil, add the broccoli rabe and
   cook until bright green and al dente, about 2 minutes. Use a
   slotted spoon to transfer the broccoli rabe to the ice bath (keep
   the pot on the grill and at a boil). When cooled, transfer the
   broccoli rabe to a kitchen towel to dry before cutting into 2-inch
   pieces.

recipe continues

5. Place a cast-iron skillet on the hot side of the grill. Add the olive oil and heat to shimmering. Add both sausage meats and cook, stirring with a wooden spoon to break up the meat, until lightly browned, about 8 minutes. Add the garlic and pepper flakes (if using) and cook, stirring occasionally, for 2 minutes, until aromatic.

6. Add the cavatelli to the boiling water and cook until they are al dente and float to the top, about 8 minutes.

7. Reserving ½ cup of the pasta water, drain the pasta and transfer to the skillet. Add the broccoli rabe and reserved pasta water and stir to combine. Remove from the heat, add the pecorino and a few twists of black pepper, and stir to combine.

8. Drizzle with some olive oil, garnish with more pecorino, and serve.

Birria-Style Beef Tacos

Serves 6

4 dried ancho chiles, halved and seeded

2 dried guajillo chiles, halved and seeded

2 dried chiles de árbol, halved and seeded

2-pound beef chuck roast

1 pound bone-in beef short ribs

Kosher salt and freshly ground black pepper

1 tablespoon extra-virgin olive oil

1 large white onion, halved

6 garlic cloves, smashed and peeled

1 medium carrot, cut into thirds

2 teaspoons dried Mexican oregano

2 teaspoons ground cumin

1 teaspoon chili powder

4 cups chicken stock

4 bay leaves, fresh or dried

12 white corn tortillas

3 cups shredded Oaxacan cheese or queso blanco

Finely chopped white onion, for serving

Roughly chopped fresh cilantro, for serving

While birria has been a mainstay in Jalisco, Mexico, for hundreds of years, it's only recently that birria tacos burst onto the taqueria scene and quickly catapulted to the top of the taco chain (thank you, social media). In towns across the country, obsessed foodies stalked their local Mexican eateries in search of this famed taco. Let me tell you: They are worth the hype—though making them is a bit of a process. While many recipes call for goat or lamb, this recipe starts with beef, which is braised slowly in a flavorful broth until very tender. The meat is shredded, tucked into tortillas with cheese, and griddled until hot, crisp, and melty. Cooking broth—or consommé—is served on the side for dipping. If you can't find melty, stringy Oaxacan cheese, sub in queso blanco, Monterey Jack, or shredded mozzarella.

1. Prepare and preheat a charcoal grill for indirect cooking, with one hot side and one hold (unheated) side. Adjust the grill vents to maintain a temperature of 275° to 300°F (see Controlling the Grill Temperature, page 17).

2. Set a large Dutch oven on the hot side of the grill. Add the ancho, guajillo, and chiles de árbol and toast, turning occasionally, until slightly charred and fragrant, about 2 minutes. Remove from the pan and set aside.

3. Season all sides of the chuck roast and short ribs with pinches of salt and twists of pepper. To the same Dutch oven, add the olive oil and heat to shimmering. Add the chuck roast and short ribs and cook, without moving, until golden brown, then turn to brown on on all sides, about 15 minutes total. Remove from the pan and set aside.

4. To the same pan, add the onion halves, garlic, carrot, oregano, cumin, and chili powder and cook, stirring occasionally, until the vegetables begin to soften, about 5 minutes. Add the chicken stock, bay leaves, and reserved toasted chiles and bring to a simmer. Return the meat to the pan and cook, partially covered, for 30 minutes.

recipe continues

5. Using tongs, carefully transfer the ancho, guajillo, and chiles de árbol to a blender, add 2 cups of stock from the pan, and blend until smooth. Return this mixture to the pan. Add 2 more cups of stock to the blender, pulse to remove any leftover chiles, and add this mixture to the pan. Cover the Dutch oven and move it to the hold side of the grill. Cover the grill and cook until the meat is very tender, about 3 hours. Top off the charcoal as needed (see Replenishing Briquettes, page 15).

6. Transfer the meats to a cutting board and carefully pull or shred the meat using two forks. Skim off most of the fat from the top of the broth and reserve it. Strain the stock through a fine-mesh sieve (discard the solids) and return the sauce to the Dutch oven to keep warm on the hold side of the grill.

7. Set a large cast-iron skillet on the hot side of the grill to preheat. Add 2 tablespoons of reserved fat to the skillet. Using tongs, dip 2 tortillas into the warm broth, coating both sides, before placing in the skillet. Top each tortilla with ¼ cup cheese followed by ¼ cup shredded beef. Cook until the cheese begins to melt, about 1 minute. Fold the tortillas in half and continue cooking until golden brown and crisp on both sides, about 1 minute per side. Remove to a plate while you repeat the process with the remaining tortillas, cheese, and meat.

8. Ladle the hot broth into small bowls, garnish with onion and cilantro, and serve with the tacos.

Clams
with Sausage and Peppers
Serves 4

4 pounds littleneck clams, scrubbed

1 pound smoked sausage, such as kielbasa, cut into ½-inch slices

3 medium red bell peppers, diced (about 3 cups)

1 small red onion, halved and thinly sliced (about ½ cup)

4 garlic cloves, thinly sliced

4 tablespoons (½ stick) unsalted butter

Kosher salt and freshly ground black pepper

1 cup chicken stock

½ cup dry white wine

⅓ cup finely chopped fresh cilantro

Clams are one of those ingredients at the fish counter that shoppers seem to look at and ignore. I get it: in their shell they don't look that inviting, and most home cooks don't have much experience preparing them. Well, I'm here to tell you that clams, like mussels, are practically foolproof! Simply toss them into some seasoned broth and steam until they pop open. Voilà! These are made in a foil pouch, so you'll want to carefully peek in near the end to make sure the clams are open. (Watch out for that hot steam when you do!) You can eat this with salad and some crusty bread or even pour it over boiled pasta.

1. Prepare and preheat a charcoal grill for direct cooking.

2. Cut off four 12 × 14-inch pieces of heavy-duty foil. Double up the foil pieces to begin forming two pouches. Dividing evenly in the center of each double-foil stack, put the clams, sausage, peppers, onions, garlic, and butter. Season each with a pinch of salt and a twist of black pepper. Lift all 4 corners of the foil up to begin to form a pouch. Before sealing, pour ½ cup chicken stock and ¼ cup wine into each packet. Tightly seal the seams of each packet.

3. When the coals are burning white, put the packets directly onto the hot coals (not on the grill grate), cover the grill, and cook until most or all of the clams have opened, about 6 minutes. Discard any clams that haven't opened after 8 minutes.

4. Carefully transfer everything to a bowl, garnish with the cilantro, and serve.

5

A Bit Fancy

When it comes to food and cooking, I would describe myself as multifaceted. I grew up in a proud blue-collar family, and many of the meals that we ate back then are still my favorites to this day. But I also went to culinary school, worked in many fine-dining restaurants, and now run a few swanky spots of my own. That tension has shaped and defined my culinary approach. If I ever get too high and mighty, though, my father is always around to say, "*Well, aren't you fancy*?!" When it comes to food, I admit that I am "a bit fancy."

The recipes in this chapter do lean a little posh, and some require a touch more finesse, but the effort always pays off in the end. A few of my favorites are the Grilled Venison Chops with Blackberry Sauce (page 181) and the Greek-Style Grilled Whole Snapper (page 186). If you've never tasted black cod, sometimes called sablefish, you must make the Spicy Black Cod with Grilled Lime (page 196). This dish improves markedly with a two-day marinade, so prepare ahead. Also in this chapter is the only crab cake recipe that you will ever need (page 173). Splurge on a good-quality tin of lump crabmeat and prepare to be wowed.

Crab Cakes
with Herby Sauce
Serves 4

Herby Sauce

1 cup mayonnaise (Duke's or Hellmann's)

½ cup buttermilk

3 scallions, white and light-green parts only, roughly chopped

½ cup fresh cilantro leaves

½ cup fresh flat-leaf parsley

¼ cup fresh dill

¼ cup fresh tarragon

Juice of 2 lemons

Kosher salt and freshly ground black pepper

Crab Cakes

½ cup mayonnaise (Duke's or Hellmann's)

1 large egg

2 teaspoons Old Bay seasoning

2 teaspoons Dijon mustard

1 teaspoon hot sauce (Frank's or Tabasco)

Grated zest and juice of ½ lime

Kosher salt and freshly ground black pepper

1 pound jumbo lump crabmeat, picked through for shells

1 cup panko bread crumbs

2 tablespoons finely chopped fresh chives

Neutral oil, for shallow-frying

There are some foods I just don't want to economize on. If I'm going to splurge on a chilled seafood tower, I want that baby overflowing with clams, oysters, shrimp, crab legs, and lobster! The same holds true for crab cakes. I would rather spend more money and leave the table satisfied than suffer through a bready, crab-scented knockoff. These, I promise, will scratch that seafood itch. Start with good-quality lump crabmeat and be super gentle when blending and forming the patties; you don't want to break up those beautiful lumps! It's also important to let them chill in the fridge for at least 1 hour (and up to overnight) so they don't fall apart during cooking.

1. Make the herby sauce: In a blender or food processor, combine the mayonnaise, buttermilk, scallions, cilantro, parsley, dill, tarragon, and lemon juice. Season with a pinch of salt and twist of pepper. Process until mostly smooth. Cover and refrigerate until needed.

2. Make the crab cakes: Line a sheet pan with parchment paper. In a large bowl, whisk to combine the mayonnaise, egg, Old Bay, mustard, hot sauce, lime zest, and lime juice. Season with a pinch of salt and twist of pepper. Use a silicone spatula to gently fold in the crabmeat, panko, and chives, being careful not to break up the lumps. Gently form the mixture into 8 equal balls and set them on the prepared sheet pan. Cover with a second piece of parchment paper, gently press the balls to form 1-inch-thick cakes, and refrigerate for at least 1 hour and up to overnight.

3. Prepare and preheat a charcoal grill for direct cooking.

4. Set a large cast-iron skillet on the grill. Line a large plate with paper towels.

5. Pour ½ inch of oil into the skillet and heat to 350°F. Working in batches so as not to crowd the pan, carefully add the crab cakes to the oil and fry until golden brown and crisp, about 3 minutes per side. Remove using a slotted spoon and drain on the paper towels.

6. Transfer to a platter, top with the herby sauce, and serve.

Plantains
with Chorizo and Roasted Tomatillo Salsa

Serves 4

4 ripe, mostly black plantains, peeled and halved lengthwise

½ pound loose fresh Mexican chorizo

¾ cup shredded Monterey Jack cheese

12 tomatillos, husked

¼ cup extra-virgin olive oil

2 jalapeños, stemmed, halved lengthwise, and seeded

2 garlic cloves, smashed and peeled

Kosher salt and freshly ground black pepper

1 cup fresh cilantro leaves

Juice of 2 limes

¼ cup Mexican crema or sour cream

This is such a fun, different, and tasty dish. It stars ripe plantains, which begin as those familiar-looking green ones but, when allowed to fully ripen, turn almost all black on the peel. Unlike the starchy version, these cook up sweet and creamy (and they are easier to peel!). Plantains are much easier to find in stores these days, but if you're having trouble, seek out the nearest Latin market. I pile on spicy chorizo and salty Monterey Jack cheese and roast them until everything comes together in a delicious, gooey package. While the plantains are cooking, I make a quick roasted tomatillo salsa to drizzle on top and serve them with cold crema or sour cream on the side.

1. Prepare and preheat a charcoal grill for indirect cooking, with one hot side and one hold (unheated) side. Adjust the grill vents to maintain a temperature of 350°F (see Controlling the Grill Temperature, page 17).

2. Arrange the split plantains on a sheet pan. Dividing evenly, top each plantain half with chorizo, pressing it into place. Sprinkle the Monterey Jack cheese on top of the chorizo. Place the pan on the hold side of the grill, cover the grill, and cook until the chorizo reaches an internal temperature of 160°F, about 15 minutes.

3. Meanwhile, set a cast-iron skillet on the hot side of the grill. In a medium bowl, toss together the tomatillos, olive oil, jalapeños, and garlic. Season with a pinch of salt and twist of pepper. Add the vegetables to the skillet, cover the grill, and cook until the vegetables are nicely charred, about 7 minutes. Carefully transfer the vegetables to a blender or food processor, add the cilantro and lime juice, and process until smooth. (If using a blender, pulse briefly at first and open the steam vent in the lid to ensure the contents don't explode!)

4. Transfer the plantains to a platter, top with the tomatillo salsa and crema, and serve.

Smoked Porterhouse
with Compound Butter
Serves 4

3-pound porterhouse steak, preferably dry-aged USDA Prime, 2½ inches thick

Kosher salt and freshly ground black pepper

8 tablespoons (1 stick) unsalted butter, at room temperature

½ cup finely chopped fresh flat-leaf parsley

1 tablespoon red wine vinegar

1 garlic clove, grated

1 brown anchovy, minced

Grated zest and juice of 1 lemon

I wrote a cookbook called *Carnivore*, so obviously I love steak! But that doesn't mean I eat expensive cuts of beef all the time; in fact, more often than not I'm grilling up skirt steaks, flank steaks, flat irons, and sirloins. But when I want to cook up something special to share with friends, I go big! Head down to your favorite butcher shop and ask them to cut you a 2½-inch-thick porterhouse steak, preferably USDA Prime. If you can find one that's been dry-aged for a bit, even better. For cuts this big and thick, you have to go reverse-sear. That's when you cook it low and slow off direct heat until it's nearly done and then blast it over the hottest coals to give it an amazing char and crust at the end. Also, make sure you take the steak out of the fridge at least 30 minutes before cooking and don't forget to let it rest before slicing.

1. Remove the steak from the refrigerator and let it sit out at room temperature while you set up the grill.

2. Prepare and preheat a charcoal grill for indirect cooking, with one hot side and one hold (unheated) side. Adjust the grill vents to maintain a temperature of 250° to 275°F (see Controlling the Grill Temperature, page 17).

3. Liberally season both sides of the steak with pinches of salt and twists of pepper.

4. In a medium bowl, stir together the butter, parsley, vinegar, garlic, anchovy, lemon zest, and lemon juice. Season with a pinch of salt and twist of pepper. Refrigerate the compound butter until needed.

5. Place the steak on the hold side of the grill, cover the grill, and cook until the steak reaches an internal temperature of 100°F, about 30 minutes.

6. Move the steak to the hot side of the grill and cook, without moving, until nicely charred on both sides, about 3 minutes per side for medium-rare (130°F), longer if you prefer more doneness.

7. Transfer the steak to a cutting board, top with the compound butter, and let rest for 10 minutes before slicing and serving.

Quick Smoked Duck Breast
with Citrus-Sesame Salad
Serves 4

Duck

1 tablespoon ground coriander

½ teaspoon ground ginger

½ teaspoon ground star anise

4 Long Island duck breasts (6 to 8 ounces each)

Kosher salt and freshly ground black pepper

Citrus-Sesame Salad

¼ cup rice vinegar

¼ cup grapeseed oil

2 tablespoons toasted sesame oil

2 tablespoons soy sauce

2 tablespoons sesame seeds, toasted

1 tablespoon Dijon mustard

Kosher salt and freshly ground black pepper

1 orange, peeled and segmented

1 grapefruit, peeled and segmented

6 scallions, white and light-green parts only, thinly sliced (about ¾ cup)

1 bunch of fresh cilantro, stemmed

It always surprises me how few amateur cooks—and even professional chefs!—prepare duck at home. Not only is it hearty, delicious, and flexible, it's less expensive than many other cuts of meat. I think a lot of the stress and fear originated from people cooking whole ducks, which can be tricky because of the large amount of fat that renders out. Duck breasts, on the other hand, are straightforward—and when smoked and seared like these, they're out of this world. You definitely want to season the duck the night before, so the aromatic spices penetrate deep into the meat. And if you want to toss a handful of wood chips (I like apple or cherry) onto the hot coals for added flavor, go for it. You can serve this dish hot or at room temperature.

1. Prepare the duck: Set a wire rack over a sheet pan. In a small bowl, whisk to combine the coriander, ginger, and star anise. Season the duck on all sides with a few pinches of salt and twists of black pepper. Season on all sides with the spice blend. Place the duck skin-side up on the rack in the sheet pan and refrigerate, uncovered, overnight.

2. Prepare and preheat a charcoal grill for indirect cooking, with one hot side and one hold (unheated) side. Adjust the grill vents to maintain a temperature of 225° to 275°F (see Controlling the Grill Temperature, page 17).

3. Place the duck skin-side up on the hold side of the grill, cover the grill, and cook until the duck reaches an internal temperature of 130°F, about 40 minutes.

4. Place the duck skin-side down on the hot side of the grill and cook until the skin is golden brown, about 2 minutes. Set aside to rest, loosely tented with foil, while you make the salad.

5. Make the citrus-sesame salad: In a medium bowl, whisk to combine the rice vinegar, grapeseed oil, sesame oil, soy sauce, sesame seeds, and mustard. Season with a pinch of salt and twist of pepper. Add the orange, grapefruit, scallions, and cilantro and toss to combine.

6. Thinly slice the duck crosswise and arrange the slices in a fan pattern on a plate. Top with the salad and serve.

Grilled Venison Chops
with Blackberry Sauce
Serves 4

Blackberry Sauce
Juice of 4 oranges
½ cup balsamic vinegar
2 tablespoons light brown
   sugar
2 tablespoons soy sauce
1 pint blackberries, halved
¼ cup finely chopped fresh
   mint leaves
¼ cup extra-virgin olive oil
1 tablespoon Dijon mustard

Venison
8 venison chops (6 ounces
   each)
2 tablespoons Dijon mustard
1 tablespoon finely chopped
   fresh thyme
Kosher salt and freshly
   ground black pepper

In the fall, during and after deer season, venison seems to pop up on seasonal restaurant menus around the country, but especially in the Midwest. I love the flavor of the dark red meat, which many describe as gamy, but I like to think of as earthy, woodsy, and wild. If you don't enjoy—or can't track down—venison, the natural swap here would be lamb chops, which offer a similar but tamer level of gaminess. But this preparation would be equally wonderful with pork chops and even baby back ribs. The savory grilled chops are topped with a sweet-tart fruit sauce starring blackberries and mint.

1. Prepare and preheat a charcoal grill for direct cooking.

2. Make the blackberry sauce: Set a medium saucepan on the grill. Add the orange juice, vinegar, brown sugar, and soy sauce and bring to a simmer. Cook until the liquid is reduced to a thick glaze, stirring occasionally, about 10 minutes. Remove from the grill and stir in the blackberries, mint, olive oil, and mustard.

3. Prepare the venison: Brush both sides of the venison with the mustard and sprinkle the chopped thyme on both sides. Liberally season both sides of the meat with salt and pepper.

4. Put the chops on the grill and cook until nicely charred on both sides and the venison reaches an internal temperature of 140°F, about 4 minutes per side. Transfer the chops to a platter to rest, loosely tented with foil, for 10 minutes.

5. Remove the foil from the platter, spoon on the blackberry sauce, and serve.

Sicilian-Style Branzino

Serves 4

½ cup dry Marsala wine

¼ cup golden raisins

2 (1-pound) branzino fillets or other firm fish (see Note)

Kosher salt and freshly ground black pepper

2 tablespoons extra-virgin olive oil

3 tablespoons unsalted butter

1 medium shallot, finely chopped

¼ cup pine nuts

2 tablespoons capers, drained

Juice of 1 orange

¼ cup finely chopped fresh flat-leaf parsley

Note: I call for branzino here, but any firm-fleshed white fish such as cod, snapper, grouper, swordfish, or sea bass would work great.

I love using a cast-iron skillet for cooking fish on the grill because you still develop a beautiful crust while avoiding the dreaded grate-stick! This is a simple dish that's loaded with big, bright Mediterranean flavors. This recipe calls for in-skillet butter basting, where you tip the pan and spoon the sauce over the cooking fish. It helps the fish to cook evenly and form a beautiful golden-brown crust. The end result is a tender, flavorful fish in a sweet, salty, buttery sauce.

1. Prepare and preheat a charcoal grill for direct cooking.

2. In a small bowl, combine the Marsala and raisins and set aside to plump up until needed.

3. Set a large cast-iron skillet on the grill to preheat.

4. Pat the outside of the fish dry with paper towels and season with a few pinches of salt and twists of black pepper.

5. To the preheated skillet, add the olive oil and 1 tablespoon butter and heat to shimmering. Add the branzino and cook, without moving, for 2 minutes. Carefully tilt the skillet and use a spoon to baste the fish while it continues to cook for 2 minutes more. Flip the fish and cook, while basting, for 2 minutes. Remove the fish from the skillet and cover with foil.

6. To the same skillet, add the shallot and pine nuts to the pan and cook, stirring occasionally, until the pine nuts begin to brown, about 3 minutes. Add the capers, orange juice, and Marsala-soaked raisins (and any remaining liquid) and bring to a simmer.

7. Remove from the grill and stir in the parsley and the remaining 2 tablespoons butter. Taste and adjust for seasoning, adding salt and pepper as needed. Place the fish on a platter, spoon the sauce over the top, and serve.

Grilled Pork Porterhouse
with Chimichurri

Serves 4

1 cup fresh flat-leaf parsley leaves

1 cup fresh cilantro leaves

6 scallions, white and light-green parts only, roughly chopped (about ¾ cup)

1 jalapeño, stemmed

2 garlic cloves, roughly chopped

6 tablespoons extra-virgin olive oil

2 tablespoons red wine vinegar

Kosher salt and freshly ground black pepper

4 pork porterhouse steaks (1 pound each)

Like their beef counterparts, pork porterhouse steaks are tender, well marbled, and deeply flavorful. And like beef steaks, they benefit from a great char over a screaming-hot grill. Don't be tempted to cook these past 145°F; they will continue to cook a little during the rest and you'd hate for them to dry out. I love to serve these with a bright and tangy chimichurri, which balances the rich and fatty pork.

1. Prepare and preheat a charcoal grill for indirect cooking, with one hot side and one hold (unheated) side.

2. In a blender or food processor, combine the parsley, cilantro, scallions, jalapeño, and garlic and pulse until coarsely chopped, about 10 times. Transfer to a bowl, add 4 tablespoons of the olive oil, the vinegar, 1 tablespoon Diamond Crystal salt, and 1 teaspoon pepper and stir to combine.

3. Drizzle the steaks with the remaining 2 tablespoons olive oil and season both sides liberally with pinches of salt and twists of black pepper. Put the steaks on the hot side of the grill and cook, without moving, until nicely charred, about 3 minutes. Flip and continue cooking until nicely charred on the other side, about 3 minutes. Move the steaks to the hold side of the grill, cover the grill, and cook until the meat reaches an internal temperature of 145°F, about 10 minutes.

4. Transfer the steaks to a cutting board, top with chimichurri, and let rest for 5 minutes before slicing and serving.

Greek-Style Grilled Whole Snapper

Serves 4

¼ cup extra-virgin olive oil, plus more for greasing
¼ cup finely chopped fresh oregano, plus 2 sprigs of oregano
1 whole red snapper (1½ to 2 pounds)
3 lemons
2 garlic cloves, sliced
Flaky sea salt
Freshly ground black pepper

The phrase "simple is often best" definitely applies to grilling seafood, especially when you're starting with a beautiful whole, just-caught fish. This straightforward approach works great with any modestly sized whole fish, so buy whatever is the freshest. In my neck of the woods, the snappers are running in late summer and early fall, so that's when I'm grilling it. You don't necessarily need special equipment, like a grill basket or fish cage to do this, but I do love how easy and stress-free it makes the grilling process.

1. Prepare and preheat a charcoal grill for indirect cooking, with one hot side and one hold (unheated) side. Brush a grill basket with olive oil.

2. In a small bowl, whisk together the ¼ cup olive oil and the chopped oregano.

3. Make three slashes ½ inch deep and 2 to 3 inches long into each side of the fish, spacing them about 1 inch apart. Thinly slice 1 lemon and place the slices, the garlic, and oregano sprigs inside the cavity of the fish. Season the cavity with a few pinches of flaky sea salt. Pat the outside of the fish dry with paper towels. Liberally apply the olive oil/oregano mixture to both sides of the fish, making sure to get it deep into the slashes. Season the fish on both sides with a few pinches of salt and twists of pepper.

4. Place the fish in the grill basket, set on the hot side of the grill, and cook until nicely charred, about 3 minutes. Flip and cook until the second side is nicely charred, about 3 minutes. Move the fish to the hold side of the grill, cover the grill, and cook until the fish reaches an internal temperature of 140°F at the thickest part, about 5 minutes. Set aside to rest, loosely tented with foil, for 5 minutes.

5. At the same time, cut the remaining 2 lemons in half and place cut-side down on the hot side of the grill. Cook, without moving, until nicely charred, about 8 minutes.

6. Transfer the fish to a platter, squeeze the grilled lemon on top, and serve.

French-Style Roasted Chicken

Serves 6

1 small bunch of thyme

Extra-virgin olive oil, for drizzling

1 whole chicken (6 pounds), cut into 8 pieces

Kosher salt and freshly ground black pepper

3 garlic cloves, sliced

½ cup sweet vermouth

1½ cups chicken stock

2 beefsteak tomatoes, cut into wedges

½ cup pitted Castelvetrano olives

3 tablespoons thinly sliced fresh basil leaves

2 tablespoons unsalted butter

This recipe comes straight out of the south of France, where bold, fresh, and simple foods are a way of life. When the landscape is this beautiful, nobody wants to spend hours cooped up in the kitchen, and there's no reason you can't take a pan-roasted chicken outside to the grill. I never grow tired of cooking whole chickens, because the possibilities are limitless, and there are always delicious leftovers. If you aren't yet in the habit of buying a whole chicken and breaking it down, you need to start! It's more economical and you have more control over the size of your bird. When you first put the chicken in the pan, don't be tempted to mess with it. Let it sear until it takes on great color and releases from the pan. That's where so much of the flavor in the pan sauce comes from!

1. Prepare and preheat a charcoal grill for indirect cooking, with one hot side and one hold (unheated) side.

2. Bundle up the thyme with a piece of butcher's twine and set aside.

3. Place a large cast-iron skillet on the hot side of the grill to preheat. Add a drizzle of olive oil to the skillet. Season both sides of the chicken with a few pinches of salt and twists of pepper. Place the chicken skin-side down in the skillet and cook until nicely charred, about 8 minutes.

4. Flip the chicken, add the garlic, and cook for 1 minute until aromatic. Add the vermouth and deglaze the pan, scraping with a wooden spoon to get up the browned bits on the bottom of the pan. Cook until the vermouth reduces slightly, about 30 seconds. Add the chicken stock, tomatoes, olives, and thyme bundle and bring to a simmer. Season with a pinch of salt and twist of pepper. Move the skillet to the hold side of the grill, cover the grill, and cook until the meat reaches an internal temperature of 165°F at the leg/thigh joint, about 20 minutes.

5. Remove the skillet from the heat and transfer the chicken to a platter. Remove and discard the thyme bundle. Stir the basil and butter into the skillet sauce. Pour the sauce over the chicken and serve.

Braised Lamb Shanks
with Gremolata
Serves 4

Braised Lamb Shanks

12 sprigs of thyme

2 sprigs of rosemary

2 bay leaves

½ cup all-purpose flour

Kosher salt and freshly ground black pepper

4 lamb shanks (1¼ pounds each)

2 tablespoons extra-virgin olive oil

2 large yellow onions, roughly chopped (about 2½ cups)

4 medium carrots, roughly chopped (about 2 cups)

4 celery stalks, roughly chopped (about 2 cups)

4 garlic cloves, minced

1 Fresno chile, seeded and minced

1 tablespoon coriander seeds

¼ cup tomato paste

1 cup dry red wine

8 cups beef stock

Gremolata

½ cup finely chopped fresh flat-leaf parsley

3 tablespoons extra-virgin olive oil

2 garlic cloves, minced

Grated zest and juice of 1 lemon

½ teaspoon kosher salt

We tend to think of braises as strictly winter fare, when we have all the time in the world to watch a big pot slowly bubble the day away. But this book is all about the grill and there is absolutely no reason why we can't transfer the process to the backyard, which is where we want to be anyway. While 3 hours sounds like a long time for a charcoal grill, it's still hours quicker than it takes to smoke a brisket. This recipe is the perfect chance to practice the snake or minion method (see page 13), which create hours of low and steady heat.

1. Prepare and preheat a charcoal grill for indirect cooking, with one hot side and one hold (unheated) side.

2. Bundle up the thyme, rosemary, and bay leaves in butcher's twine and set aside.

3. Prepare the braised lamb shanks: Place the flour in a large bowl and season with a pinch of salt and a twist of pepper. Season the lamb on all sides with pinches of salt and twists of pepper. Dredge the lamb in the seasoned flour, making sure to coat all sides well. Shake off the excess.

4. Set a large enameled Dutch oven on the hot side of the grill. Add the olive oil and heat to shimmering. Working in batches, if necessary, add the lamb and cook until golden brown on all sides, turning as each side finishes, about 15 minutes. Use a slotted spoon to transfer to a plate when done.

5. To the same Dutch oven, add the onions, carrots, celery, garlic, chile, coriander, the herb bundle, and 1 teaspoon Diamond Crystal kosher salt and cook, stirring occasionally, until the vegetables begin to soften, about 5 minutes.

recipe continues

6. Add the tomato paste and cook, stirring occasionally, until the paste begins to darken, about 2 minutes. Add the wine and deglaze the pan, scraping with a wooden spoon to get up the browned bits on the bottom of the pan. Add the beef stock and taste and adjust for seasoning, adding salt and pepper as needed. Return the lamb shanks to the sauce, cover, and move to the hold side of the grill. Cover the grill and cook until the lamb is fork-tender, about 3 hours. Top off the charcoal as needed (see Replenishing Briquettes, page 15).

7. Meanwhile, make the gremolata: In a medium bowl, stir together the parsley, olive oil, garlic, lemon zest, lemon juice, and salt. Let sit at room temperature for 30 minutes before serving.

8. Transfer the lamb shanks to a platter. Remove and discard the herb bundle. Carefully transfer the sauce to a blender or food processor and process until smooth. (If using a blender, pulse briefly at first and open the steam vent in the lid to ensure the contents don't explode!)

9. Pour the sauce over the lamb shanks, top with gremolata, and serve.

Halibut Piccata

Serves 4

8 tablespoons (1 stick)
   unsalted butter, at room
   temperature
¼ cup finely chopped fresh
   flat-leaf parsley, plus
   ½ cup whole leaves
2 tablespoons salt-packed
   capers, rinsed
Grated zest and juice of
   1 lemon
2 garlic cloves, grated
½ cup all-purpose flour
Kosher salt
3 large eggs
1 tablespoon Dijon mustard
½ teaspoon hot sauce
2 cups panko bread crumbs
4 halibut fillets (6 ounces
   each)
Freshly ground black pepper
Extra-virgin olive oil, for
   shallow-frying and
   drizzling
½ cup dry white wine
½ cup chicken stock
½ cup thinly sliced radishes

In East Hampton, there's a place called Bostwick's Chowder House, a casual seafood spot beloved by locals and visitors alike. Bobby Flay and I have been going there for years, and it's where I always end up taking friends who visit me on the East End. While I love everything on the menu (I'm looking at you, hot-buttered lobster roll!), I rarely pass up the fluke Milanese. The seafood out there is truly amazing, with fresh catch rolling in every day. If you've never tasted fresh fluke, you should seek it out—it's firm, mild, and sweet. This recipe is inspired by my favorite dish at Bostwick's, but I swap out the fluke for the more accessible halibut. If you can find fresh fluke (or flounder), go for it. If not, you can also substitute sole, cod, or haddock.

1. Prepare and preheat a charcoal grill for indirect cooking, with one hot side and one hold (unheated) side.

2. In a medium bowl, stir together the butter, chopped parsley, capers, lemon zest, lemon juice, and garlic.

3. Set up a dredging station in three shallow bowls: Put the flour in one bowl and season with a pinch of salt. In a second bowl, whisk together the eggs, mustard, hot sauce, and a pinch of salt. Put the panko in the third bowl and season with a pinch of salt.

4. Pat the fish dry with paper towels and season on both sides with a pinch of salt and twist of pepper. Working with one piece of fish at a time, dredge the fish in the flour, making sure to coat both sides well. Shake off the excess. Dip the fish into the beaten eggs, allowing the excess to drip off. Finally, lay the fish in the panko, turning and pressing to fully coat both sides.

5. Line a large plate or platter with paper towels. Pour ½ inch of olive oil into a large cast-iron skillet and set it on the hot side of the grill.

6. When the oil is shimmering, carefully add the fish and cook until golden brown and crispy on both sides, about 3 minutes per side. If the oil is getting too hot, slide the pan off the heat. When done, transfer the fish to the paper towels.

recipe continues

7. Carefully pour the oil out of the skillet (reserving for another use) and return the pan to the hot side of the grill. Add the wine and cook until reduced by half, about 1 minute. Add the chicken stock and cook until reduced by half, about 1 minute. Add the butter/parsley mixture and cook, whisking constantly, for 1 minute.

8. In a small bowl, combine the parsley leaves and radishes. Drizzle with olive oil and toss to combine. Transfer the fish to a platter, spoon over the sauce, top with the parsley/radish salad, and serve.

Spicy Black Cod
with Grilled Lime

Serves 4

¼ cup dry sake
¼ cup mirin
3 tablespoons sugar
2 tablespoons sriracha
¼ cup white miso paste
1 tablespoon rice vinegar
4 skin-on black cod fillets
  (6 to 8 ounces each)
2 limes, halved
Kosher salt, for sprinkling

Black cod, also known as sablefish, is one of the heathiest and most delicious fishes out there. It's mild, sweet, and flaky and loaded with omega-3 fatty acids. Because it's such a mild-flavored fish, it plays well with marinades and sauces. This version, made with sake, mirin, and miso, results in a pleasantly sweet and savory fish loaded with umami. The longer the fish marinates the better it will taste, so consider making the marinade a few nights ahead of time when you're already grilling something else. An overnight marinade is good, but when you go for two—or even three—days the fish is off the charts.

1. Prepare and preheat a charcoal grill for direct cooking.

2. Set a small saucepan on the grill. Add the sake, mirin, sugar, and sriracha and bring to a simmer, whisking frequently. Remove from the grill and whisk in the miso and vinegar. Set aside to cool.

3. Put the cod in a shallow dish. When the miso mixture has cooled, pour over the cod, cover, and refrigerate for at least 1 day and up to 3 days.

4. Prepare and preheat a charcoal grill for indirect cooking, with one hot side and one hold (unheated) side.

5. Remove the cod from the marinade, allowing most of it to drip off. Discard the marinade. Place the fish skin-side down on the hold side of the grill. Cover the grill and cook until the fish is flaky and completely cooked through, about 10 minutes.

6. Meanwhile, sprinkle the limes with salt, place cut-side down on the hot side of the grill, and cook, without moving, for 5 minutes.

7. Transfer the fish to a platter, squeeze the limes over the fish, and serve.

Planked Everything Bagel Spiced Salmon

Serves 6

1 cedar plank large enough
to accommodate the
salmon
1 (2-pound) salmon fillet,
skin and pin bones
removed
3 tablespoons Dijon mustard
½ cup everything bagel
seasoning

On the east side of Cleveland, "everything bagels" are rightly called "mish-mosh bagels." If you grew up going to Bialy's Bagels, which has been around longer than me, or any of the Jewish delis in town that carried their products, you wouldn't even know what the heck an everything bagel was! But the last I checked, you can't find Mish-Mosh Bagel Seasoning on store shelves, so here we are. That said, this addictive blend (typically sesame seeds, dried onion, dried garlic, poppy seeds, and sea salt) is great on *everything*! I love putting it on salmon, which to me feels like a play on the classic deli pairing of bagels and lox. Serve this with the Spicy Cucumber Salad (page 43).

1. Soak the cedar plank in water for at least 30 minutes.

2. Meanwhile, prepare and preheat a charcoal grill for indirect cooking, with one hot side and one hold (unheated) side. Adjust the grill vents to maintain a temperature of 350°F (see Controlling the Grill Temperature, page 17).

3. Brush the salmon with the mustard on one side and then top with the everything bagel seasoning. Put the salmon seasoning-side up on the cedar plank, place it on the hold side of the grill, cover the grill, and cook until the fish reaches an internal temperature of 125°F, about 25 minutes.

4. Plate the fish and serve.

Fire-Pit Steak and Potatoes

Serves 4 to 6

2 pounds baby Yukon Gold potatoes

3 sprigs of rosemary, plus 2 tablespoons finely chopped fresh rosemary

3 garlic cloves, sliced

4 tablespoons extra-virgin olive oil

Kosher salt and freshly ground black pepper

½ cup dry white wine

2 rib-eye steaks, 2 inches thick

Flaky sea salt, for serving

Here's a fun twist on the famous reverse-sear technique. After cooking the steaks over indirect heat as one would normally do, we sear them not *over* the hot coals but *on* them. You read that correctly: We drop those suckers right onto the white-hot charcoal. Not only is this method impressive to behold, it produces the most incredible crust imaginable while imparting intense wood-grilled flavor. I've found that very little charcoal transfers to the steaks during the sear, but if some does, simply brush it off. These potatoes are completely hands-off easy, roasting slowly in the coals while the steaks are cooking.

1. Prepare and preheat a charcoal grill for indirect cooking, with one hot side and one hold (unheated) side. Adjust the grill vents to maintain a temperature of 300°F (see Controlling the Grill Temperature, page 17).

2. Cut off two 12 × 14-inch pieces of heavy-duty foil and stack them together. In the center, put the potatoes, rosemary sprigs, garlic, and 2 tablespoons of the olive oil. Season with a pinch of kosher salt and twist of pepper. Lift all 4 corners of the foil up to begin to form a pouch. Before sealing, pour the white wine into the packet. Tightly seal the seams of the packet. Use a knife to poke a few holes in the top of the pouch to vent steam. When the coals are burning white, put the packet directly onto the hot coals (not on the grill grate) and cook until the potatoes are tender, about 30 minutes. Put the grill grate back in place for the steaks.

3. Meanwhile, in a small bowl, stir together 2 tablespoons Diamond Crystal kosher salt, 2 tablespoons pepper, and the chopped rosemary. Liberally season both sides of the steaks with this mixture. Put the steaks on the grill grate on the hold side of the grill, cover the grill, and cook until the meat reaches an internal temperature of 120°F for rare to 130°F for medium (the steaks will cook to 125°F or 135°F, respectively, on the coals), about 30 minutes.

4. Remove the steaks from the grill and carefully remove and set aside the grill grate. Slide the potato packet to one side of the coals. Brush the steaks on both sides with the remaining 2 tablespoons olive oil and place directly onto the hot coals. Cook until well charred, about 3 minutes per side. Transfer to a cutting board, loosely tent with foil, and set aside to rest for 10 minutes before slicing.

5. Remove the potatoes from the grill and carefully transfer them to a bowl. Season with flaky sea salt and serve with the steak.

Smoky Grilled Shrimp

Serves 6

3 tablespoons extra-virgin
   olive oil
Grated zest and juice
   of 2 limes
1 tablespoon Diamond
   Crystal kosher salt
1 tablespoon light brown
   sugar
1 tablespoon smoked
   paprika
1 teaspoon cayenne pepper
1 teaspoon ground
   coriander
1 teaspoon ground cumin
2 pounds large shrimp,
   peeled and deveined
½ cup fresh cilantro leaves,
   for serving
Lime wedges, for squeezing

When it comes to surefire seafood for groups, it's hard to top shrimp. Even for people who say they don't love seafood, shrimp seems to be the exception. The plump, sweet crustaceans are the perfect carrier for any flavor combination you feel like going with—and they grill up in no time flat! I like to use head-on shrimp when they're available because I love the presentation—and I think they taste better! These require at least an hour of marinating time, but they cook in less than five minutes. To prevent sticking to the grill, make sure the grates are preheated, scrubbed clean, and oiled before laying these guys down. If you would prefer to skewer them before cooking them, go right ahead.

1. In a medium bowl, whisk together the olive oil, lime zest, lime juice, salt, brown sugar, smoked paprika, cayenne, coriander, and cumin. Add the shrimp and toss to fully coat. Cover and refrigerate for at least 1 hour and up to 4 hours.

2. Prepare and preheat a charcoal grill for direct cooking.

3. Cook the shrimp on the hot side of the grill until nicely charred, about 2 minutes per side.

4 Transfer the shrimp to a platter, garnish with cilantro leaves and lime wedges, and serve.

6

With Coffee

As much as I love cooking, I've never professed to be much of a dessert-maker. Dessert-eater? You betcha! When we entertain, those duties typically land in Lizzie's lap. Unlike me, she has the patience required for the "sweeter arts." I've always enjoyed a little something sweet at the end of a big meal, but I find that the older I get, the more I crave dessert with my post-meal coffee.

Most of the desserts that we make at home—and most of the ones in this chapter—aren't sugar bombs, though. We adore recipes like Frozen Raspberry and Lime Pie (page 207) and Peaches and Cream (page 227), which rely on fruit for their sweetness as opposed to heaps of processed sugars. If you have a backyard firepit (or even some hot coals in the barbecue) and love cooking desserts like s'mores, you should definitely look into buying something called a pie iron or toastie maker. These long-handled cast-iron gadgets are a blast to use, especially when making delicious meal-cappers like Campfire Nutella-Banana Sandwiches (page 222).

Obviously, many of the baked desserts in this chapter can be made indoors, but the whole point of this cookbook is to illustrate the broad functionality of a simple charcoal grill. And think of the look on your guests' faces when you pull a perfectly baked Chocolate Bundt Cake (page 221) from your trusty backyard cooker!

Frozen Raspberry and Lime Pie

Serves 8

Crust

2 cups graham cracker crumbs

8 tablespoons (1 stick) unsalted butter, melted

¼ cup packed light brown sugar

Grated zest of 3 limes (juice reserved for filling)

1 teaspoon Diamond Crystal kosher salt

Filling

5 cups fresh raspberries, divided

1½ cups whole-milk Greek yogurt

½ cup granulated sugar

Juice of 3 limes

8 ounces mascarpone cheese

¼ cup raw honey

1 teaspoon pure vanilla extract

1 teaspoon pure almond extract (optional)

1½ cups heavy cream, divided

In the summertime, I'm always experimenting with no-bake desserts that are simple to prepare, but still feel special. This one is bursting with bright fruit flavor, with the lime juice and zest somehow making the raspberries taste sweeter. The hardest part of this entire recipe is waiting the couple hours for the pie to freeze before enjoying!

1. Make the crust: In a medium bowl, stir together the graham cracker crumbs, melted butter, brown sugar, lime zest, and salt. Transfer this mixture to a 9-inch springform pan and use a 1-cup measuring cup to evenly press the mixture onto the bottom and one-third of the way up the sides of the pan.

2. Make the filling: In a blender or food processor, combine 4 cups of the raspberries, yogurt, granulated sugar, and lime juice and process until smooth. Transfer to a medium bowl, add the mascarpone, honey, vanilla, and almond extract (if using), and whisk to combine. In a separate medium bowl, whisk the cream until it holds medium peaks, about 6 minutes. Use a silicone spatula to gently fold one-third of the cream into the raspberry mixture. Cover and refrigerate the remaining whipped cream.

3. Pour the filling into the pie crust, cover with plastic wrap, and freeze until firm, about 3 hours. Top with whipped cream, garnish with remaining 1 cup of raspberries, slice with a warm knife, and serve.

Chocolate Chip Cookie Bars

Makes 24 bars

Softened butter, for the
baking pan
2 cups all-purpose flour
1 teaspoon baking soda
¾ teaspoon kosher salt
12 tablespoons (1½ sticks)
unsalted butter, at room
temperature
1 cup packed light brown
sugar
½ cup granulated sugar
2 large eggs
2 teaspoons pure vanilla
extract
2 teaspoons maple syrup
18 ounces bittersweet
chocolate, cut into small
chunks (about 3 cups)
Flaky sea salt, for serving

One of my all-time favorite snacks growing up was Chips Ahoy!
cookies and an ice-cold glass of milk. I'm not embarrassed to
admit that occasionally I'd eat the entire bag and drink a whole
carton of milk! My love affair with chocolate chip cookies hasn't
waned a bit, although my cookie of choice has matured a little.
When I'm craving homemade cookies but don't have the time or
energy to form all those little balls, I make these bars. Not only is
this method easier and quicker, but the bars stay moist and gooey
for longer. Maple syrup lends a subtle nuttiness without having
to add nuts. I love topping a warm bar with some cool, creamy
vanilla bean ice cream!

1. Prepare and preheat a charcoal grill for indirect cooking, with
   one hot side and one hold (unheated) side. Adjust the grill vents
   to maintain a temperature of 350°F (see Controlling the Grill
   Temperature, page 17).

2. Grease a 9 × 13-inch metal baking pan or grill-safe ceramic
   baking dish with butter.

3. In a medium bowl, whisk together the flour, baking soda, and
   kosher salt.

4. In a stand mixer fitted with the paddle, combine the butter,
   brown sugar, and granulated sugar and beat on low speed until
   combined. Increase the speed to medium and beat until thoroughly
   combined, about 5 minutes. Add the eggs one at a time and
   beat until fully incorporated. Add the vanilla and maple syrup
   and beat until incorporated. Add the flour mixture and beat until
   well blended, stopping once or twice to scrape down the sides
   and bottom of the bowl, about 2 minutes. Set aside one-third of
   the chopped chocolate and stir the remaining chocolate into the
   dough until incorporated. Evenly press the dough into the prepared
   baking pan and top with the reserved chopped chocolate.

5. Place the pan on the hold side of the grill, cover the grill, and
   bake until golden brown and a toothpick inserted into the center
   comes out clean, about 30 minutes.

6. Remove from the grill and sprinkle with flaky salt. Let cool for
   10 minutes before cutting into bars and serving.

Fresh Strawberry Pie

Serves 6

Crust

1 cup graham cracker crumbs

4 tablespoons (½ stick) unsalted butter, melted

3 tablespoons granulated sugar

½ teaspoon kosher salt

Filling

2½ pounds strawberries, hulled and quartered (about 8 cups)

⅓ cup granulated sugar

¼ cup cornstarch

2 tablespoons strawberry preserves

Kosher salt

1 tablespoon fresh lemon juice

Topping

1 cup heavy cream

1 tablespoon powdered sugar

1 teaspoon pure vanilla extract

Fresh strawberries, for topping

Berries don't last long in our garden. If they don't get picked off by birds, chipmunks, or bunnies, they are nibbled straight off the vine, bush, or cane by humans (especially small ones!). If by some miracle we find ourselves with a bumper crop of early summer strawberries, I make this wonderful pie. Not only is it bursting with summer goodness, it's ridiculously easy to put together. My grandkids Emmy and Butchie both go crazy for it and I'm sure your family will, too.

1. Prepare and preheat a charcoal grill for indirect cooking, with one hot side and one hold (unheated) side.

2. Make the crust: In a medium bowl, stir together the graham cracker crumbs, melted butter, granulated sugar, and salt to combine. Scrape the mixture into a 9-inch springform pan and use a 1-cup measuring cup to evenly press the mixture onto the bottom and one-third of the way up the sides of the pan. Set the pan on the hold side of the grill, cover the grill, and bake until golden brown, about 15 minutes. Let the crust cool while you make the filling.

3. Make the filling: Measure out 2 cups of the strawberries (setting the rest aside in a large bowl) and place in a small saucepan. Use a potato masher to crush the strawberries to a chunky sauce. Add the granulated sugar, cornstarch, strawberry preserves, a pinch of salt, and 1 tablespoon water and bring to a boil on the hot side of the grill. Cook, stirring occasionally, until the sugar dissolves, about 2 minutes. Pour this mixture over the bowl of reserved strawberries, add the lemon juice, and stir to combine.

4. Pour the filling into the pie crust and smooth the surface with a silicone spatula. Cover and refrigerate until set, at least 4 hours, or up to overnight.

5. Make the topping: In a stand mixer fitted with the whisk, combine the heavy cream, powdered sugar, and vanilla and whisk on medium speed until the cream holds soft peaks, about 3 minutes.

6. Spread the topping evenly on top of the pie, slice, and serve garnished with fresh strawberries.

Kyle's Chocolate Cake Donuts

Makes 8 donuts

Cooking spray
1¾ cups sour cream
1⅓ cups granulated sugar
5 large egg yolks
3 tablespoons unsalted
    butter, at room
    temperature
2 teaspoons pure vanilla
    extract
2 cups all-purpose flour,
    plus more for rolling and
    shaping
1¾ cups cake flour
1 cup unsweetened cocoa
    powder
3 teaspoons baking powder
2 teaspoons Diamond
    Crystal kosher salt, plus
    more as needed
Neutral oil, for deep-frying
3 cups powdered sugar
½ cup whole milk
Sprinkles (optional), for
    garnish

When Kyle opened Grindstone Donuts in Sag Harbor in 2016, he sold only naturally risen brioche-style donuts. The three-day process is not for the faint of heart, but the light, airy, irresistible donuts fly off the shelves, often selling out by early afternoon. After about a year in business, he listened to his clientele and began testing cake-style donut recipes to add to the mix. He soon landed on this chocolate donut recipe—and it's become a café staple. (It's my granddaughter Emmy's favorite, too.) And because nobody should waste perfectly good chocolate donut dough, we fry up the donut holes as well. These are best hot and fresh out of the fryer, but they also are surprisingly good when baked (about 12 minutes at 350°F).

1. Grease a large bowl with cooking spray.

2. In a stand mixer fitted with the paddle, beat the sour cream, granulated sugar, egg yolks, butter, and vanilla on low speed until combined. Increase the speed to medium and beat until well blended, about 2 minutes.

3. Sift the all-purpose flour, cake flour, and cocoa powder into a medium bowl. Add the baking powder and salt and whisk to combine. Add the flour mixture to the wet ingredients in the mixer and beat on low until just combined, stopping once or twice to scrape down the sides and bottom of the bowl, about 3 minutes.

4. Transfer the dough to the greased bowl, cover tightly with plastic wrap, and refrigerate until needed, but not longer than 4 hours.

5. Prepare and preheat a charcoal grill for direct cooking. Lightly flour a sheet pan.

6. Pour 6 inches of neutral oil into a heavy deep-bottomed pot (about 2 quarts), set on the grill, and heat to 350°F. Set a wire rack over a sheet pan.

7. On a lightly floured surface, roll out the dough to a ¾-inch thickness. Flour a 3-inch donut cutter and cut out the donuts by pressing straight down without twisting. Transfer the donuts and donut holes to the prepared sheet pan.

8. Working in batches, add the donuts and donut holes to the hot oil and fry until lightly golden on both sides, about 2 minutes per side. When done, use a slotted spoon or spider strainer to transfer the donuts to the rack.

9. In a medium bowl, whisk to combine the powdered sugar, milk, and a pinch of salt until the sugar is fully dissolved and the glaze is smooth.

10. When the donuts are cool enough to handle, dip the top of the donuts in the glaze, letting any excess drip off. Top with sprinkles, if desired, and serve.

Chocolate Pudding and Pretzel Pie

Serves 8

Crust

1 cup finely ground pretzels

1 cup ground chocolate wafers

8 tablespoons (1 stick) unsalted butter, melted

2 tablespoons light brown sugar

Filling

2½ cups whole milk

¼ cup granulated sugar

3 tablespoons raw honey

6 large egg yolks

2 tablespoons cornstarch

1 teaspoon instant espresso powder

1 teaspoon Diamond Crystal kosher salt

8 tablespoons (1 stick) unsalted butter, cut into small cubes

8 ounces bittersweet chocolate, roughly chopped, plus more for garnish

Whipped cream, for serving

To me, there is no better flavor pairing for a dessert than salty and sweet. Hats off to the French chocolatier who first dreamed up salted caramel, the pinnacle of the salty-sweet confection world. This simple no-bake pie (except for the pretzel and chocolate wafer crust) is always a huge crowd pleaser. The contrast between the buttery-sweet and creamy chocolate filling set against the salty-crisp pretzel crust is one for the ages. I recommend you make the crust the day before, when your grill is on anyway . . . then finish off the pie and keep it in the fridge until dinner (or whenever!) the next day.

1. Prepare and preheat a charcoal grill for indirect cooking, with one hot side and one hold (unheated) side. Adjust the grill vents to maintain a temperature of 350°F (see Controlling the Grill Temperature, page 17).

2. Make the crust: In a medium bowl, stir together the pretzel crumbs, chocolate wafer crumbs, melted butter, and brown sugar. Transfer the mixture to a 9-inch springform pan and use a 1-cup measuring cup to evenly press the mixture onto the bottom and one-third of the way up the sides of the pan.

3. Place the pan on the hold side of the grill, cover the grill, and bake until firm, about 10 minutes.

4. Make the filling: Set a medium saucepan on the hot side of the grill. Add the milk, granulated sugar, and honey and bring to a simmer. Remove from the heat. In a large bowl, whisk together the egg yolks, cornstarch, espresso powder, and salt until smooth. Whisking constantly, slowly add half of the hot milk mixture to the egg mixture. Pour this warmed egg mixture into the saucepan with the remaining milk and whisk to combine. Return the saucepan to the hold side of the grill and stir with a silicone spatula, scraping the bottom and sides of the pot, until thickened and small bubbles form on the surface, about 5 minutes. Remove from the heat, add the butter and chocolate, and whisk until melted and incorporated. Pour the filling into the baked pie crust, cover, and refrigerate for at least 4 hours and up to overnight.

5. Slice with a warm knife, top with whipped cream and shaved chocolate, and serve.

Ginger Cookies

Makes 24 cookies

2 cups sugar, plus more for rolling

12 tablespoons (1½ sticks) unsalted butter, at room temperature

¾ cup vegetable shortening

½ cup molasses

2 large eggs

4½ cups all-purpose flour

3½ teaspoons baking soda

2 teaspoons ground cinnamon

1½ teaspoons ground ginger

1½ teaspoons ground cloves

½ teaspoon freshly grated nutmeg

½ teaspoon kosher salt

This recipe comes courtesy of my friend Albert Fiero, who got it from his friend, who got it from his friend, and so on. Not only do I love the story behind the cookies, I adore the cookies. These chewy ginger cookies are so easy to make that my grandkids could practically do it all on their own. (Except for the baking part.) The dough comes together in a jiffy and it's so much fun forming them into little ball shapes and rolling them in sugar. Bake these just until cracks begin to form on the surface of the cookies.

1. Prepare and preheat a charcoal grill for indirect cooking, with one hot side and one hold (unheated) side. Adjust the grill vents to maintain a temperature of 350°F (see Controlling the Grill Temperature, page 17).

2. In a stand mixer fitted with the paddle, beat the sugar, butter, shortening, molasses, and eggs on low speed to combine. Increase the speed to medium and beat until pale and fluffy, about 5 minutes. Sift the flour into a medium bowl, add the baking soda, cinnamon, ginger, cloves, nutmeg, and salt and whisk to combine. Add the flour mixture to the butter mixture and beat on low until well blended, stopping once or twice to scrape down the sides and bottom of the bowl, about 2 minutes.

3. Put some sugar in a shallow bowl. Divide the dough into 24 equal portions and roll each into a walnut-size ball. Working with a few balls at a time, roll the balls in the sugar, making sure to coat all around. Transfer to an unlined sheet pan.

4. Place the pan on the hold side of the grill, cover the grill, and bake until the surface of the cookies crack, about 10 minutes. Remove from the grill and set aside to cool for 10 minutes and serve.

Sweet Corn Panna Cotta

Serves 4

2 ears of corn

1¼ cups whole milk

1 (¼-ounce) envelope
   unflavored gelatin powder

⅓ cup sugar

1 teaspoon Diamond Crystal
   kosher salt

1 cup crème fraîche

2 teaspoons pure vanilla
   extract

Fresh blueberries, for serving

I can practically hear the comments in my head as I write this: "Corn in dessert?!" To all the doubters out there I say, try it before you decry it! Summer corn is naturally sweet, and the flavor is so distinctive that it's instantly recognizable. I like to keep the ingredient under wraps so I can watch as guests take their first bites, smile, and identify the mystery flavor. This is a great dessert for entertaining—especially alfresco-style—because it can be made up to two days in advance. Just wait to garnish them with fruit until before serving.

1. Prepare and preheat a charcoal grill for direct cooking.

2. With a sharp knife, remove the kernels from the ears of corn. Reserve the kernels for another use (such as Creamed Corn with Lime on page 72). Snap the corncobs in half and add to a medium saucepan along with the milk. Place on the grill and bring to a simmer. Remove from the grill, cover, and let steep for 20 minutes. When cool enough to handle, scrape the cobs with the back of a knife to release the milky liquid into the saucepan.

3. Meanwhile, add 3 tablespoons cold water to a small saucepan. Sprinkle the gelatin on top and let sit for 5 minutes to hydrate.

4. Place the saucepan with the corn/milk mixture on the grill and bring to a simmer. Add the sugar and salt and whisk to dissolve. Remove from the heat.

5. Place the saucepan with the gelatin on the grill and cook until dissolved, whisking frequently, about 5 minutes. Stir this mixture into the sweetened milk along with the crème fraîche and vanilla.

6. Pour into four 8-ounce ramekins, cover, and refrigerate until set, at least 3 hours, or up to overnight.

7. Serve chilled and topped with fresh blueberries.

Chocolate Bundt Cake

Serves 10

Cooking spray
1 cup cake flour
⅔ cup all-purpose flour
2 tablespoons unsweetened cocoa powder
1 tablespoon instant espresso powder
½ teaspoon baking soda
3 ounces bittersweet chocolate, roughly chopped
16 tablespoons (2 sticks) unsalted butter, at room temperature
1 cup sugar
3 large eggs
½ cup honey
1 cup boiling water

Everybody's favorite "cake with a hole in it," Bundt cakes are an enduring favorite on the dessert table. I love the look of a perfectly baked Bundt cake, with all those sexy curves, waves, and valleys. One of the signature features of a Bundt is the glaze on top, but this cake is so rich, delicious, and chocolaty that no glaze is required. Pour a nice tall glass of cold milk and prepare to be elated.

1. Prepare and preheat a charcoal grill for indirect cooking, with one hot side and one hold (unheated) side. Adjust the grill vents to maintain a temperature of 350°F (see Controlling the Grill Temperature, page 17).

2. Grease a 10-inch Bundt pan with cooking spray.

3. In a large bowl, whisk together the cake flour, all-purpose flour, cocoa powder, espresso powder, and baking soda.

4. Set a saucepan on the hot side of the grill and bring 1 inch of water to a boil. Set a heatproof bowl over the saucepan (make sure the bottom of the bowl doesn't touch the hot water) and add the chocolate. Stir until completely melted and smooth, about 3 minutes.

5. In a stand mixer fitted with the paddle, beat the butter and sugar on low to combine, then increase to medium and beat until pale and fluffy, about 5 minutes. Reduce the speed to medium-low and add the eggs one at a time, beating well after each addition until fully incorporated. Add the honey and melted chocolate and beat until incorporated, about 2 minutes. Reduce the speed to low, add the flour mixture, and beat on low to medium-low until well blended, stopping once or twice to scrape down the sides and bottom of the bowl. While beating, slowly add the boiling water until incorporated.

6. Pour the batter into the prepared Bundt pan. Place the pan on the hold side of the grill, cover the grill, and bake until a toothpick inserted into the center comes out clean, about 1 hour. Top off charcoal as needed (see Replenishing Briquettes, page 15).

7. Remove from the grill and set aside to cool for 20 minutes before removing from the pan, slicing, and serving.

Campfire Nutella-Banana Sandwiches

Serves 4

Cooking spray
4 tablespoons Nutella
8 slices soft white bread, like Pullman or milk bread
2 bananas, each halved lengthwise and then crosswise (8 pieces total)

Everybody loves a good s'more—especially my grandkids. There are a million and one ways to improvise and customize the classic formula (if you've never swapped the chocolate bar for a Reese's Peanut Butter Cup, you don't know what you're missing!). This twist is especially fun because we get to bust out the old-fashioned pie irons. These cast-iron gadgets resemble little waffle irons on a long stick, and they can go directly onto the hot embers. If you're looking for an excuse to add a couple to your grilling kit, know that you can make amazing savory snacks in them, too, such as the world's best grilled cheese toasties!

1. Prepare and preheat a charcoal grill for direct cooking.

2. Liberally grease the inside of the pie iron(s) with cooking spray.

3. Divide the Nutella evenly among 4 slices of the bread. Top each slice with 2 banana slices. Top with remaining slices of bread.

4. Place the sandwiches in the pie iron(s), close the lids, and trim off and discard any excess bread. When the coals are burning white, put the irons directly onto the hot coals (not on the grill grate) and cook for 2 minutes per side—at this point, they should be golden brown and toasty.

5. Transfer the irons to a cutting board, carefully remove the sandwiches, cut in half, and serve.

Peaches and Cream

Serves 4

3 very ripe peaches
2 cups heavy cream
3 tablespoons powdered
  sugar
2 tablespoons honey
1 teaspoon pure vanilla
  extract
8 shortbread cookies,
  4 whole, 4 crumbled
Grated zest of 2 limes
Fresh mint leaves, for garnish

When you find yourself with peaches that are excessively ripe, make this incredibly easy dessert. The night before you want to make it, just pop a handful of whole peaches—skins and all—into the freezer. When shredded on a simple box grater, the frozen fruit is transformed into a summery and refreshing peach-flavored granita. While wonderful on its own, I like to pair the frozen treat with buttery shortbread cookies and vanilla-kissed whipped cream.

1. The night before serving, place the whole peaches in the freezer (washed but unpeeled).

2. When ready to serve, in a medium bowl, whisk the cream, powdered sugar, honey, and vanilla until the cream holds medium peaks, about 6 minutes.

3. Grate the frozen peaches around the pit on the large holes of a box grater. Place 1 whole cookie into the bottom of each of four 6-ounce glasses. Divide the grated peaches among the glasses. Top with the whipped cream, garnish with lime zest, fresh mint, and crumbled cookies, and serve.

7

Drinks

Liz and I love to entertain, but the last thing either one of us wants to do is be cooped up *inside* messing with complicated cocktails while all the fun is happening *outside*. That's why we love the batch cocktail! Just like the name sounds, these easy-to-prepare drinks are constructed by the pitcher, with enough volume for four servings in each recipe. If you are entertaining groups larger than that, simply double or triple the ingredients to make a larger batch. Keep the pitcher on ice or in the fridge so it's nice and cold when serving—and don't forget to make plenty of ice ahead of time.

Many of the drinks in this chapter are refreshing slushie-style cocktails that require a little advance planning, such as making flavored ice cubes or popping some fruit in the freezer the night before. But other than that, they come together in a jiff, leaving more time to spend with your friends enjoying the cocktails!

Also, if you've never tried a BBC—short for Baileys Banana Colada— prepare to discover your new favorite summer refresher!

Frozen Mango and Pineapple Sangria

Makes 4 cocktails

1 (750 ml) bottle Sauvignon Blanc

2 cups chopped frozen mango

2 cups chopped frozen pineapple

¼ cup maple syrup

Juice of 4 limes (about ½ cup)

Mint sprigs, for serving

Lime wheels, for serving

This is like the slushie version of white sangria. We start with a nice bottle of Sauvignon Blanc and load up the blender with frozen pineapple and mango. You can substitute simple syrup for the maple syrup, but I love the subtle depth of flavor it adds to the drink. Again, this recipe is easily scaled up for bigger batches.

In a blender, combine the wine, frozen fruit, maple syrup, and lime juice and blend until smooth and slushy. Pour into chilled glasses or insulated tumblers, garnish with mint and a lime wheel, and serve.

Frozen Strawberry Salty Dog

Makes 4 cocktails

Kosher salt

Lemon wedges

2 cups pink grapefruit juice

1 cup vodka, chilled

1 cup frozen strawberries

½ cup fresh lemon juice
(2 to 3 lemons)

4 whole strawberries, for
garnish

When you wind up with a bunch of strawberries approaching max ripeness, place some in a bag and pop them in the freezer. All it takes is a cup of frozen strawberries to make these refreshing drinks. (You can also use frozen berries from the store.) I like these with vodka, but they are just as good when made with gin.

1. Spread some kosher salt in a small dish (wide enough to accommodate the rim of a cocktail glass). Moisten the rims of cocktail glasses with lemon wedges, then dip the rims into the dish with salt and twist to coat the rims. Set aside.

2. In a blender, combine the grapefruit juice, vodka, frozen strawberries, and lemon juice and blend until smooth and slushy. Pour into the salt-rimmed glasses, garnish each with a strawberry, and serve.

Paper Plane

Makes 4 cocktails

¼ cup bourbon
¼ cup Aperol
¼ cup amaro, such as
   Montenegro or Nonino
¼ cup fresh lemon juice
   (1 to 2 lemons)
Ice cubes
Orange zest, for serving

The Paper Plane looks and tastes like a classic, classic cocktail, but it's a relatively modern invention. Sam Ross, the man behind the drink, created it for Violet Hour in Chicago. I've been on a bit of a Paper Plane kick lately—and I have zero regrets! The recipe can't be any simpler as it's four ingredients, equal parts of each one.

In a cocktail shaker, combine the bourbon, Aperol, amaro, and lemon juice. Add ice, cover, and shake vigorously for 15 seconds. Strain into cocktail glasses, garnish with orange zest, and serve.

Frozen Lime G&Ts

Makes 4 cocktails

1 liter tonic water
1 cup limeade
1 cup gin
Grated zest of 1 lime
Lime wedges, for serving

If you don't identify as a bona fide gin lover, turn the page! This boozy bevvie is the ideal pool-side refresher, brightened up with a good dose of lime zest. Don't forget to make the limeade ice cubes the night before.

1. The day before serving, in a large pitcher, combine the tonic and limeade and stir to blend. Pour into ice cube trays to freeze into cubes. When frozen, pop the cubes out of each tray and store in separate zip-top bags in the freezer for up to 1 week.

2. In a blender, combine the limeade ice cubes, gin, and lime zest and process until smooth and slushy. Pour into chilled glasses or insulated tumblers, garnish with lime, and serve.

Peach Sangria

Makes 6 cocktails

1 pound ripe peaches, sliced
1 (750 ml) bottle dry
  Riesling
¾ cup Grand Marnier

If you're like me, you tend to go overboard at farmers' markets, bringing home way more fruit than you can possibly eat. If it happens to be peach season when that occurs, make a big batch of this summer treat. This recipe is great for large groups, and it can be made a couple hours in advance if kept in the fridge.

In a 2-quart pitcher, combine the peaches, wine, and Grand Marnier. Cover and refrigerate for 1 hour. Pour into chilled glasses or insulated tumblers, garnish with peaches from the pitcher, and serve.

Baileys Banana Colada (BBC)

Makes 4 cocktails

3 bananas, sliced
½ cup canned full-fat
  coconut milk
½ cup Baileys Irish Cream
¼ cup dark rum
2 teaspoons instant coffee
1 cup ice cubes

Out here on the East End, these drinks are called, simply, BBCs. Despite being hopelessly out of fashion, Baileys Irish Cream is making the rounds again thanks to this irresistible cocktail. These rum-soaked drinks start with frozen bananas and are finished with coconut and coffee. Use the best dark rum you can find—and if you're feeling a little rowdy, top the finished drinks with a rum floater. To do that, slowly pour a shot of rum over the back of a spoon, with the tip of the spoon just touching the surface of the drink, so that the booze floats on top of the drink.

1. The day before, place the bananas in a zip-top bag in the freezer and freeze overnight.

2. In a blender, combine the frozen bananas, coconut milk, Baileys, rum, coffee, and ice cubes and process until smooth.

3. Divide into glasses and serve.

A
Fix It with Food
Index for Recipes in
Symon's Dinners Cooking Out

RECIPE	PAGE	FLOUR-FREE	DAIRY-FREE	MEAT-FREE
Grilled Flank Steak with Pepper Relish	105	X	X	
Ultimate Italian Hoagies	106			
Smoky Portobello Cheesesteaks	109			X
Oysters Casino	110			
Pan-Fried Mozzarella Sandwiches with Tomato Salad	112			X
Sloppy Joe Tacos	115		X	
Smoked Trout with Arugula, Dill, and Lemon	116		X	X
Quick Marinated Grilled Scallops	119	X	X	X
Grill-Roasted Cauliflower with Lime Vinaigrette	120	X	X	X
Grilled Swordfish with Salsa Fresca	123	X	X	X
Gyro-Style Lamb Burgers with Tzatziki and Grilled Onion	124			
Skillet-Grilled Chicken Piccata	129	X		
Grilled Chicken Souvlaki	130	X	X	
City Chicken Skewers	133		X	

RECIPE	PAGE	FLOUR-FREE	DAIRY-FREE	MEAT-FREE
Meatball Parmesan Sandwiches	137			
Beef and Potato Casserole	138			
Coney Dogs	141		X	
Symon's Juicy Lucy Double Cheese and Bacon Burger	142			
Eggs in Heaven	144			
Stuffed Tomatoes	145			
Spatchcock Chicken	147	X	X	
Crispy Feta Eggs	148			X
Slow-Grilled Pork Butt Steaks with Cherry BBQ Sauce	151	X	X	
Pastrami-Smoked Pork Belly	155	X	X	
Fettuccine with Smoked Tomato Sauce	156			X
Grilled Eggplant Parmesan	159	X		X
Mom's American Dish	160			
Cavatelli with Sausage and Broccoli Rabe	163			
Birria-Style Beef Tacos	165	X		
Clams with Sausage and Peppers	168	X		

A BIT FANCY

RECIPE	PAGE	FLOUR-FREE	DAIRY-FREE	MEAT-FREE
Crab Cakes with Herby Sauce	173			X
Plantains with Chorizo and Roasted Tomatillo Salsa	174	X		
Smoked Porterhouse with Compound Butter	177	X		
Quick Smoked Duck Breast with Citrus-Sesame Salad	178	X	X	
Grilled Venison Chops with Blackberry Sauce	181	X	X	
Sicilian-Style Branzino	182	X		X
Grilled Pork Porterhouse with Chimichurri	185	X	X	
Greek-Style Grilled Whole Snapper	186	X	X	X
French-Style Roasted Chicken	189	X		
Braised Lamb Shanks with Gremolata	190		X	
Halibut Piccata	193			
Spicy Black Cod with Grilled Lime	196	X	X	X
Planked Everything Bagel Spiced Salmon	199	X	X	X
Fire-Pit Steak and Potatoes	200	X	X	
Smoky Grilled Shrimp	203	X	X	X

Acknowledgments

I wouldn't be where I am today without the love, trust, and support of my wife, Liz, who has always been so understanding about the demands of work and travel. The same goes for Mom, Dad, and my grandparents, who inspired in me not only a love for food but also an appreciation for people and how those two ingredients come together when entertaining. Much love to Kyle, Krista, Emmy, and Butchie. Having them in my life—and nearby—not only inspires me but also fills my life with a degree of meaning and joy that I didn't realize was possible.

This year, Liz and I lost two of the most important people in our lives: her mom, Sherla, and my father, Dennis. The strength, guidance, and love that they instilled in us will never be forgotten. They both inspired the way we live. Their zest for life and their love of entertaining, being the life of the party, and spending time outdoors with the people they love is the spirit of this book. We love and miss you both.

Boundless thanks and appreciation is owed to culinary director Tim Connors, whose meticulous recipe testing guarantees that every dish in this cookbook will come out perfectly time after time. His forty-plus years of friendship also mean the world to me.

I owe so much to Scott Feldman of Two-Twelve Management, my manager of nearly twenty years. Not only is he a fierce representative of my career, but he also happens to be a gentleman and a true friend. His mastery of the food and media world is unmatched. Thanks also to Margaret Riley King with William Morris Agency, who not only has become a trusted ally in my professional endeavors but also has become a great friend and creative muse.

Thank you to my Food Network family for allowing me to teach, inspire, and entertain home cooks for the better part of twenty years. Your confidence in me resulted in the creation of *Symons Dinner's Cooking Out* in the middle of a pandemic! From those humble beginnings emerged this very cookbook.

This is the eighth cookbook that I've collaborated on with Douglas Trattner, my gifted—and patient—coauthor who keeps these projects on track despite my challenging schedule.

I'm fortunate to have the privilege of working alongside Ed Anderson, one of the most talented food photographers in the game today. Together with Maeve Sheridan, the team does a brilliant job of capturing the true personality of the food while creating a consistent look and feel throughout. These books wouldn't be half as good without Anderson's eye and skill.

I also had the honor and pleasure once again to collaborate with Susan Spungen, a true legend in the world of food styling. Her attention to detail improves my books in a million and one ways. It's always a joy to work with Susan and her team, which includes Danielle Marin, Matteo Connolly, and Cammie Blaszak.

Last but certainly not least, I owe so much thanks and credit to Raquel Pelzel, our unflagging—and unflappable—editor at Potter. Her goal always is to produce the very best cookbook possible—and she has been doing that for me for more than half my cookbook-writing career.

Index

CLARKSON POTTER/PUBLISHERS
An imprint of the Crown Publishing Group
A division of Penguin Random House LLC
clarksonpotter.com

CLARKSON POTTER is a trademark and **POTTER** with colophon is a registered trademark of **Penguin Random House LLC.**

Library of Congress Cataloging-in-Publication Data
Names: Symon, Michael, 1969- author. | Trattner, Douglas, author. Anderson, Ed (Edward Charles), photographer. Title: Symon's dinners cooking outside / Michael Symon and Douglas Trattner ; photographs by Ed Anderson. Identifiers: LCCN 2024026558 | ISBN 9780593797648 (hardcover) | ISBN 9780593797655 (ebook)
Subjects: LCSH: Outdoor cooking. | Dinners and dining. | LCGFT: Cookbooks.
Classification: LCC TX823 .S994 2025 | DDC 641.5/78—dc23/eng/20240907
LC record available at https://lccn.loc.gov/2024026558

ISBN 978-0-593-79764-8
Signed edition ISBN 979-8-217-03411-6
Ebook ISBN 978-0-593-79765-5

Editor: **Raquel Pelzel**
Editorial assistant: **Elaine Hennig**
Art director and designer: **Ian Dingman**
Production editor: **Natalie Blachere**
Production manager: **Jessica Heim**
Compositors: **Merri Ann Morrell** and **Zoe Tokushige**
Photographer: **Ed Anderson**
Food stylist: **Susan Spungen**
Food stylist assistants: **Matteo Connolly** and **Danielle Marin**
Prop stylist: **Maeve Sheridan**
Copyeditor: **Kate Slate**
Proofreader: **Rachel Holzman**
Indexer: **Elizabeth Parson**
Publicist: **Jina Stanfill**
Marketer: **Stephanie Davis**

Manufactured in China

10 9 8 7 6 5 4 3 2 1

First Edition